TABLE OF CONTENTS

PART ONE: A GROWING COMMUNITY PROBLEM

CHAPTER 1

BASTION ON THE HILL (A STATE OF THE ART OPERATION)

Tenacity is the spark that made our ancestors come to America and eventually migrate across the continent. It is that spark that makes Americans stand up against overwhelming odds. It is the same spark that made a small, poor community of just 300 individuals in California stand up against the corporate, industrial, and political interest of distant Los Angeles County and their influence over local county, state, and federal health departments and regulators. The road ahead would be daunting for this non-affluent community, but tenacity knows no bounds.

Above the small, serene community of Casmalia, high on a hill about one mile from our community's school yard, sat the site of one of Southern California's largest toxic dump sites. One of the tributaries of the Casmalia Creek started at the middle of the site and wound its way down the hillside close to the back of our State School District's property, where it joined another tributary that came from the front of the site's main gate and then snaked its way to the Pacific Ocean after joining behind the school property. These streams were normally dry, but in the rainy season, they became torrents of gushing water headed to the ocean.

The property behind the school had not always been a toxic waste site but had grown from an unnoticed, innocuous beginning on rolling ranch lands as a waste dump for oil field waste slowly into its present form with the addition of new state permits and county approvals.

The dump owner bought out neighboring complaining ranch owners until he owned thousands of acres. Unfortunately, the dump site was not located in the center of the vast property but was next to the community. Initially, most residents of the town were unaware of its existence. As awareness grew with the noxious fumes that its growing size emitted, the community found that the site was protected by an invisible wall built upon falsehoods perpetuated by all levels of government regulators and political interests. The invisible scam's wall that stood above the community like a medieval bastion was protected by the vested interests of individuals, regulatory boards, and factual myths. The individuals, boards, and myths needed to be hammered and hammered until this invisible wall came crashing down. To accomplish this feat, the community needed to pull together as one to meet the challenges that lay ahead.

RELUCTANT WARRIOR

I must admit, at first, I was a disbeliever in the need for any action as I came to work each day from what seemed to be far off Orcutt, but I was a loyal employee and followed directions. My directions came from my superiors, our three-member school board composed of locals from the small community. Unlike larger state school districts that had five board members, ours functioned with just the three individuals who met each month in our modern well-equipped multi-purpose room. This room and school building were in stark contrast to the rest of the rough and tumble community. As usual, our meetings were carried out at this location without other community members present, as other community members had ample opportunity in the small community each day to share concerns with each member. Our board president was James Postiff, a handicapped individual who worked during the day as a civilian employee at neighboring Vandenburg Air Force Base. He had the stamina to successfully push on and raise a small family despite his handicap. He had much difficulty, as usual, entering the room that afternoon because of his childhood hunting and gun injuries that had left one leg and arm mostly immobile. After a cordial round of greetings, our meeting began on time after James called it to order with the customary flag salute. They were fed up with nighttime-generated odors and fumes from our unwanted neighbor, and the meeting soon zeroed in on the proposed letter to the EPA on the agenda. It soon became clear, after comments from the members, that the board wanted to move forward with a letter concerning the neighboring dump site, and so our long journey of confrontations began from this rather casual beginning.

In June of 1981, at the direction of the board of trustees and in my capacity as principal/superintendent of the small school district, I composed a letter and board resolution to the San Francisco office of the U.S. Environmental Protection Agency in opposition to the proposed expansion of our neighboring toxic dump site. It was the first of many communications concerning the dump site. Although this letter was done with great care, my heart and interest were not in favor of this effort. At the time, to me, it was just a road sign saying Casmalia Resources. I passed on the winding highway at the intersection of NTU Road as I came to school in the morning and left in the evening. It was a distant problem that I was personally erroneously sure was being supervised by federal, state, and county authorities. It was also a distant problem for me because I was busy raising my small family and running, as a broker, my six-sales agent real estate office after work each day until 9:00 in the evening and on weekends in neighboring Old Town Orcutt. Fortunately, I sold my real estate office to an associate prior to the full impact of the looming dump confrontation and activities. It was a busy life for both me and my new blond, beautiful wife, Pernelle, who at that time worked as a teacher in the neighboring Orcutt Union School District, as well as raising our own two children. Luckily, we made enough together to afford a nanny to help out with the children as they grew.

Another factor that made it difficult for me to support this effort was a community activist who ranted and raved against the dump site. He was a person who reminded me of Moe in "The Three Stooges." Moe was cubby in appearance, and he fit the description of Moe in all details. He had two associates in Santa Maria that specialized in unsubstantiated water well testing. I am sure all their hearts were in the right place, but they did not inspire a lot of confidence because of their similar poor demeanor. News reporters had shared with me the fact that Moe, in his description of health effects, had rolled around on the hood of an auto, pretending to have a reaction to toxic exposure. An overweight adult moaning on top of a car hood did more harm than good for the community's cause. Wisely, I kept my distance from these individuals through the course of coming events, always worked with other community members, and avoided direct involvement with the three.

Marsha Davis should have been my "canary in the mine shaft," but again, I failed to take note. Marsha was a young, new teacher, fresh out of Cai-Poly in San Luis Obispo, who eventually became beloved by all the students. I can vividly remember her at her employment interview in my office. On her paper work, she far out-showed the other applicants. Her angel-like appearance and demeanor caught my attention immediately, and I felt she would be a strong asset for the school with her friendly, good nature and calm temperament. Her piercing eyes sealed the employment deal. Later in her employment, on trips into the classroom, I was always amazed at how well she interacted with the children. She was the perfect teacher, but her tenure was to be short-lived!

Marsha lived with her new husband in San Luis Obispo. They were both in excellent health and were avid bike riders who thought nothing of traveling from San Luis Obispo to Santa Barbara, passing by Casmalia and the dump site on bike rides on weekends. I am sure their joint outstanding health brought them together in the world. One particular weekend, they detoured off the main road, riding down to the dump's main gate. The following Monday, she quizzed me about the dump site.

At the time, to my later chagrin, I had no problem with the site and conveyed no alarm to her.

During the next summer break, she came down with a blood disorder, leukemia, and passed away in a hospital in Santa Barbara at the beginning of the next school year. I was shocked to hear the news from her husband that she would not be back the following school year. Again, I still failed to put her condition and the dump site together. Perhaps I could just not face the realization of the danger to the entire community and school.

Even though Marsha had been with us for only a short period of time, her death was a shock to the entire school when I announced it after her short absence at the beginning of the school year. Her new husband, understandably, was crushed by the chain of events. I had much difficulty telling the schoolchildren what had happened to her and can remember fighting back my emotions in trying to explain why a young, healthy person would die at such a young age.

Months after her death, I received a polite call from her husband with inquiries similar to Marsha's after her bike trip to the entrance of the dump. He, too, was trying to make up for his loss. Tears came to my eyes as I spoke to him on the phone, and I tried to mask the emotion in my voice. Again, not being an expert, I had no hard evidence to tie the dump site and her death together. We were far away from the chemical industries in the Eastern United States, which were accustomed to dumping toxic waste into rivers, with the resulting health issues for nearby workers and residents. Marsha's husband was suspicious, and so was the community.

I must admit it gave me great satisfaction a few years later when the community's attorney started the process of legal action against the site, and I had to dig up the whereabouts of Marsha's husband and parents for the legal paperwork. I, at last, felt somewhat relieved that I finally had an answer to their questions when I relayed on the phone the community's decision to finally sue the site. Although no one could bring Marsha back, it was a pleasure to get her family's new address and ask them to join in the suit! It was also later a pleasure to use Marsha's photo and likeness as a symbol of community resistance to the dump site on an informational video to get our point of view out to the public!

I kept my memories of Marsha and my false doubts to myself and diligently did my best work learned in law school for the district on the EPA letter. The community was concerned about the winter overflows into the stream bed behind our school site. The purpose of our letter and resolution was to oppose the dump's recent application to expand the site by 14.08 acres to accommodate more highly toxic waste in unlined lagoons, which had been declared unsafe by a committee of Congress. The letter listed our concerns: the failure of the dump owner to operate the facility in a safe manner during a 1978 overflow of contaminants into the watershed adjacent to school property; the failure of any one agency to be primarily responsible for the safe operation of the site; the need for an independent geologic report; the warning of irreparable damage to the water basin as well as harm to adjacent property owners by the Santa Barbara County Planning Commission; and the failure of local authorities to investigate potential hazards to citizens and public school students adjacent to the site.

But the most important portion of the letter contained the following: "In addition, the board has directed me to secure legal counsel for the district to better represent their position." Quickly, on Aug. 26, we were notified by the EPA that the dump owner, Mr. Hunter, had withdrawn his application for expansion. A small victory, but only the first of many more confrontations and additional problems!

On April 22, 1983, I also prepared a letter to the Board of Supervisors supporting a 10% county tax on all income from the toxic dump site. It was the school board's view that the income could be used to protect the public from potential health and safety hazards.

Little did they know at the time of the large amount of money that would be coming into Casmalia Dump Site in future years or of the efforts by the dump site to increase the volume and flow of toxic material, but none of the additional income would be used to protect the community. This tax eventually made it more difficult for the county to break away from the influence of the dump because they were, in effect, sharing in the profits.

GREED, GREED, AND MORE GREED

Unknown to the community and kept secret by county regulators, the dump owner was slowly increasing the dump's ability to take in additional waste. Major toxic dumps in Los Angeles County were being prepared for closure because of contamination of the environment and water tables in those valleys. Cash from the Federal Superfund would be used for the transport and storage of waste from the LA areas to other dumps around the state. The amount of money to be made was staggering. Hunter, the dump owner, eyes were aglow with dollar signs. He just needed more space. Because of the district's and others' opposition, he had abandoned the idea of expanding by 14.08 acres, but this would not stop his efforts. There were other means to get rid of waste faster. He could not flush it down the creek as he had done in the past as the State Water Board frowned on this method and he had been ordered to keep it on site, but he could expand by what he called "scientifically as Enhanced Aeration," which was, in fact, just plain old enhanced evaporation using ordinary farming irrigation pipe and sprinklers. This he slowly expanded to cover the entire area on all hill sides of the permitted areas. Later, I found all this was done under the eyes of county air pollution inspectors without any permits.

Next, he made arrangements for the Zimpro Wet Air Oxidation System, which in essence heated waste of all kinds and spewed toxic steam into the air. Boy! Could you get rid of waste using this unproven and untested method? The community and public were unaware of all these issues and techniques, but the dump owner was now ready for the gold rush from the clean-up of Southern California's toxic dumps.

COMMUNITY CONDITIONS WORSEN

Starting in August 1984, the situation started to worsen as families began having more severe problems with the fumes and odors at night, resulting in nausea, headaches, and eye irritation. It slowly started drifting in during the daytime hours, thus making it a school problem and, unfortunately, my problem. By October 26, 1984, the board was fed up and directed me to contact Kenneth Nelson, County Counsel, for an injunction. Being a small district, we were provided legal service by the County Counsel's Office, which also provided legal service to the Board of Supervisors and all county departments. This arrangement made the situation ripe for a legal conflict of interest. Larger school districts had their own law firms. My letter was intended to be a confidential letter to our school district's attorney, the county counsel, so I was dismayed by the person who answered my confidential letter in great detail. But the person who answered showed me the close connection between the County of Santa Barbara and the pull and sway of the dump site owner, the local oil and gas industry, and the faraway Southern California industry and associated politics.

The letter came from one of the largest law firms in Santa Barbara County, with approximately twenty-two associates. The question became: how did they get a copy of a private communication to our district's attorney? What in the world were county personnel doing, sharing this request with a company they should be regulating? The letter, in effect, was rather comical because it threatened to sue both me personally and the district generally for asking our attorney to look into an injunction! The underlying message was for us, and me in particular, to shut up.

My response to this outrageous letter was just the opposite of what they wanted. The letter made my blood boil and awakened something deep within me, but I did manage a controlled response to this absurd threat. My response was loud and shook the vested establishment in the county. I sent a letter to Dr. Lawrence Hart, the county health director, asking for an immediate emergency investigation of the health problems at our school that were disrupting normal school activities. In addition, I asked for an immediate meeting with him and his staff to discuss the problem and, in particular, ask if his department had appropriate testing equipment and how many people from his department could be assigned to the problem. But the real importance of the letter was who received a copy of it first! I told my secretary to send a copy of the letter to the Santa Barbara Newspress days before it was mailed to Dr. Hart, with a note asking that it be placed on the front page. The newspaper obliged, so I am sure the large law firm got the message. I never heard from them again. But I did hear from Dr. Hart, as he apparently did not like to first read his mail in the newspaper. But that was alright because he or his staff or the county counsel's staff, I am sure, was responsible for inappropriately forwarding my original confidential letter about the injunction along to the dump owner. From that time forward, I had a cool relationship with the health director, which was fine with me.

Naturally, I was later curious as to who had forwarded the confidential request to the dump owner. So, when I was on the phone with a deputy county counsel concerning regular school business, I asked him what had happened in reference to the toxic dump injunction. I got a straight answer: "You are not playing ball as you have teed off all the county officials. Hey, Ken, this isn't the way we do it in Santa Barbara County". This attitude of protecting industry and showing no sympathy for the poor carried through with most future contacts with the county. It was clear that the county was so entwined with the dump site and local industry that they could not function as regulators. Slowly, ever so slowly, the twists and turns of current and future events would turn me from a reluctant warrior into an aggressive environmental activist!

CHAPTER 2

CRISIS AND CONFRONTATIONS

EMERGENCY CLOSURE

I arrived as usual on a November day in 1984, an hour or so before other employees, so I could take care of my duties as principal/superintendent without interruptions. It was a sunny but cool morning as the coastal fog started to dissipate from the coastal community and school grounds. Unlocking the steel gate to the school grounds, I headed to my office to get started. The pungent, sweet, disgusting smell of chemicals from the toxic dump site was in the air, which had surely been worse during the nighttime hours with the usual wave of coastal fog that swept in from the sea each afternoon and up the canyon to the community and school. The fog appeared to hold the fumes down next to the ground in the canyon. Being sure there would again be reports from students and parents about the extent of the nighttime fumes as they arrived to line up at the classroom door, it took some effort to attempt to put the bad fumes issues out of mind, although this mental exercise each day was becoming more difficult as the reports to me increased in volume and intensity of their nighttime distress and the overall impact on their school work. Busying myself with needed school district paper work, my early morning passed by quickly.

Meg Gyll, my jovial, loyal school secretary, who always managed to keep my spirits up, arrived a bit early on this day. She had a keen sense of humor, and I always enjoyed her duplicate letters, one humorous as well as another that was actually dictated. The humorous one stated what she thought needed to be said in not-so-diplomatic terms. For example, she would place her version of a letter to various health officials with many well-deserved names and obscenities on my desk on top of the real one. We had many great times and laughed together through the years. Today was not to be such a happy day.

At school starting time, all school employees were at their assigned locations, and students were lined up at the doors to each classroom, with some parents who had walked their students to school standing back to make sure they got to school safely. After a hearty "good morning, students", in unison, I got a "good morning, Mr. McCalip" in return. Students entered the classrooms. The entire school then, again, assembled in front of the school for the flag raising and the pledge, which had become the tradition in the small school district. Back inside, I did receive fume reports about the prior night, but I encouraged students to leave that behind as we had to focus on the day's school work. The morning went well except that I did receive a report from the outside recess aide that fumes seemed to be worse today. Not having been outside, I just responded with, "keep an eye on it at the next recess period". It still did not seem to be a serious day-time school problem to me, but events that day would cause this view to change forever.

Lunch time at our school was different than in most state schools. In this small rural community, all students just walked home for lunch or ate a free lunch and then walked home. I ate lunch in my office while working on rough drafts of state school reports that would soon become due. Then, walking through the school library and into the large school multi-purpose room, I noted some of the heating units were still running from the cooler morning hours. It was time these were turned off, so a quick exit was made through a side door to the exterior of the building. Our school was relatively new and had been built while I was away at law school, with large modern mansard overhangs that covered sidewalks around the entire building. As I made my way to the electrical room to turn off the heat in the back of the building, it dawned on me that the outside odors were extremely bad, worse than I had ever experienced. There was zero wind and not the usual ocean breeze coming up the canyon. The fumes were thick and bad, like nothing I had before confronted. Perhaps now I knew what the community experienced at night when I was snug, miles away, at home. The mansard overhang had captured the thick, toxic brew from our unwanted neighbor. Fumbling with keys to open the door, I began to notice that I was having difficulty getting a breath of air. By the time I exited the electrical room, I realized that there was no breathable oxygen in the air. I tried to hold my breath to avoid breathing the toxic mixture, but this maneuver proved unsuccessful, and I was forced to inhale a large lung full of the airborne materials. Toxic fumes on this day, because of climate conditions, had settled under the mansard eves of the school building. My head was now pounding with an instant, severe headache. Quickly entering the side door to the multi-purpose room, I sat down at the nearest table and put my head down in my folded arms on the table as I felt faint and disorientated. "Mr. McCalip, are you feeling OK?" was the next thing I heard from the teacher, who had just entered the room from her adjacent classroom.

DECISION TO CLOSE

Slowly lifting my head off the table and explaining what had just happened and adding, "I have decided to close the school under emergency conditions as we all need to leave the community. Students need to be sent home so parents can take them out of the area if they wish. Do you agree?" A hardy, unhesitating "yes", was the answer, and we quickly started the process of closing the school. Most students were still at home for lunch or on the way back to school. Meg started calling down our list of parents, and I directed her to check off and make sure each parent was contacted. It was at this moment that I realized we had a serious problem and that my personal period of denial needed to stop. The community activist, despite his lack of finesse, was correct. My head was now continuing to pound with a serious and unusual headache. Fortunately, our brick-structured school building shielded us from the bulk of the toxic fumes that morning as we hurriedly prepared to abandon ship!

I then made two fast courtesy calls. The first one was to the Santa Barbara County Superintendent of Schools office to let them know we were closing under emergency conditions. Bill Cirone, the superintendent, was gone for lunch, so a startled receptionist took the message. Next, I called the Santa Barbara County Counsel's office to quickly explain the situation. A young county counselor was the only person in the office at lunch time. Again, I asked, do you concur with the closing? There was a moment of hesitation, but he answered yes. Both contacts were told I could not stay on the line long, as we needed to call parents quickly and exit the location, and they would not be able to reach me at the school number, as the school would be in lockdown, but they could reach me at home later in the afternoon, as I was not feeling well, and would be at my doctor's office. No call was made to the air pollution control district, which was a subdivision of the county health department, because they had in the past contended in their usual contemptuous manner with community members, as well as me, that they could not verify even the source of the odors and fumes even though they had inspectors on site. Later, we were told by experts that even a five-year-old child could have accomplished this task. They obviously had some other unknown agenda.

SHORT RESPITE

All notifications to parents were made, and we locked the front gate to the school, and we all headed toward home. I first headed to my private doctor in the Orcutt area in the adjacent Santa Maria Valley. It was a relief to be leaving, but I had worries about the students who would be at home in Casmalia under similar conditions as existed at the school that day.

Even though I had no appointment, Dr. Luca's staff let me in immediately and started taking my vital signs. Dr. Luca was an extremely competent physician from Eastern Europe, and he always impressed me with his keen interest in his patients' health as he always carefully listened to what you said. I explained what had transpired and that I had been exposed to a hodgepodge of highly toxic chemicals, but I had no clue as to what they were. On this day, I went from perfect health to instant, extremely high blood pressure. Dr. Luca was unable to provide much other help because he did not know the specific chemicals. But he did not want me back in the work environment. I explained that I would try to stay away as long as I could, but I had a small family to provide for. Later, during the next six years, he treated me for off-and-on bronchial asthma, which lasted for two or three weeks at a time, would clear up for a week or so, and then be back again with a vengeance. My instant high blood pressure was to continue for the rest of my life, but medications kept it under control. It was the start of a downward trend for everyone's health in the small community!

After picking up medication at the drug store, I spent the rest of the day trying to rest up at home, but this was to be a short respite. Little did I know that an emergency closure of a public school generates local and national attention. Phone calls started to pour in from the county health department wanting a meeting with me, local and national media, and others. I let the answering machine handle these, and later in the day, my wife let them know I was under a doctor's care and was not available.

I finally started returning calls. The first of these was to my employer, James Postiff, the president of the board of trustees. He assured me that they were one hundred percent in favor of the closure. I in turn explained that the health department was wanting to meet with me and that my plan was to try to negotiate some health and safety assurances before I would reopen the school. He concurred with this strategy.

I next returned the call from Dr. Laurence Hart, the county health director, whom I now despised because of our earlier exchange of letters and his refusal to provide any support to the school district or community, but I kept the conversation cordial. He was a medical doctor with a British accent that made him come across as even more condescending. His desire was to convene a task force of his staff to meet with me at the school. My first reaction was, "How about some other location?" I finally relented, and the meeting was set for the following week at the school. In my head, I was pondering, "Why did the pompous ass not send the task force in response to my letter to him asking for help in the Santa Barbara News Press?" But I kept my thoughts to myself!

PHYSICAL CONFRONTATION AND TASK FORCE MEETING

Other than the odors and fumes on the drive out from the Santa Maria Valley through the hills and past the toxic dump site entrance, the day of the meeting was a clear, sunny day with no fumes or odors around the school facility. When I arrived, an entourage of county vehicles was parked in front of the school. I opened the gate and the school's front door, and we all, including a couple of representatives from Casmalia, proceeded to the school's multi-purpose room for the meeting. The multi-purpose room in which I had fond memories of many Christmas events held within it now brings back terrible memories of fleeing from it on the recent closure day. Dr. Hart and his motley crew of so-called health professionals found seats around one of the tables. He proceeded to introduce each of his staff, which consisted of about five county employees, to me and the others, in what to me now was his arrogant British accent. I am sure my feelings were based on our earlier confrontations and his lack of help and support for the community. When he reached Mr. English, the head of the air pollution district, I asked him if he and I could meet after the meeting in my private office. This was agreeable to him. I intended to merely get more specific information, but my intentions changed as the task force meeting proceeded and my emotions kicked in!

Again, the county officials tried to convince us that they had no "scientific" way of telling where the odors and fumes were coming from since we also had oil fields in the area. Perhaps with air testing, it could be traced back to the toxic dump site. I responded that this denial of the obvious insulted both my intelligence and the community's. I went on to explain that the standard response from the Air Pollution Control Department was to first deny that any odor even existed, but if numerous calls were received, then to jump to an inability to determine the source of the fumes. This response was the same rehearsed response from the top officials down to the lowly site inspectors. I explained that community members had actually walked the short mile to the site and could smell the same odors that existed in the community coming from the ponds of waste. Dr. Hart and others on his crew explained that the only way they could take action was to track it down with a scientific test of the air, and the air test he had planned would be in our best interest. This issue was left unresolved.

After this first item, the meeting moved uncomfortably on to school safety. I informed them that I would not be reopening the school unless we received a county employee, such as a county nurse, to be present during the school day. It was not to be a county school nurse, but a person on their payroll. This was to be a discussion and dispute that continued for several weeks. Dr. Hart agreed, but the issue of who was to pay for it was to be settled at a later date. I also asked for air testing to begin. Dr. Hart tentatively agreed with the nurse to check into air testing. Next, they were informed by me that from this day forward, the school would be operated on a day-to-day basis, and if the school staff and I felt it was unsafe, it would be shutdown. Under my calm school principal demeanor, I was seething with anger at both Dr. Hart and Mr. English caused by the chain of events and the prior confrontations with Dr. Hart!

I managed to remain cool and cordial through the group meeting. I thanked each county employee with a handshake and a goodbye as they left and then Mr. English and I slipped into my private office.

As soon as the door shut in my private office, all my pent-up rage and emotions erupted. Mr. English was the primary person in charge and responsible for running schoolchildren out of the public school under what appeared to be lax supervision. Before I knew it, Mr. English was up against the wall with his feet dangling above the floor. Cuss words flowed from my mouth: "God Dam it, Mother Fucker", as I asked him, what type of person would let this happen to small, helpless schoolchildren? then I made the following threat, not knowing how in the world I would carry it out: "Let me assure you, I don't know how, but one way or another, I am going to make sure you are eventually fired and are no longer with the county." I then released my grip, and he slid down the wall and made a fast exit from the school building. In my view, he was a worm of a human and not entitled to any respect.

Walking over and crashing down in my office chair, I tried to compose myself and my shaking body, as this expression of anger was out of my usual character and I had never lost it before. Perhaps my outburst was from my Cherokee or Scottish backgrounds, or perhaps both. I always projected and maintained an attempt at calm and composure, but perhaps my response was well deserved and appropriate for the existing situation. It was months later that I learned that Director English, soon after our confrontation, did not ever return to work for the county. This mystified me, as, although a tall person, I am sure I was not that terrifying. What secret was he hiding, and what nerve did I strike?

At home that evening, I made no mention to my wife or anyone else about my behavior at the private meeting in my office that day. On the first day of school, four days later after the closure, the health department nurse arrived on time, and our school day started on time. It was a wonderful day with no fog and bright sunshine. There was not a hint of toxic fumes.

CHAPTER 3

REFLECTIONS

(FATE. YOUTH, WAR, LOVE AND MARRIAGE)

Sitting at my desk in the principal's office after the confrontation, my mind started to wonder as I pondered my earlier life and how I arrived in the small, dusty town of Casmalia, not only once but twice, and what I should do next in relation to the toxic dump problem and my future. Casmalia sits where a Chumash Indian village once existed, and its Chumash Indian name means "The Last One," presumably because of its far-off location in the coastal foothills. Looking at it in 1984, you would have thought you had been transported back in time to an early western town. During the early 1900's, many famous early movie stars got off the Coastal Rail Line at its depot in Casmalia for a buggy ride to the Marsallia Dude Ranch close by on what is now Vandenburg Air Force Base. The old rail depot has long since been turned into another small shanty, and the old cattle corrals to load cattle onto the rail line are long gone. The Air Force Base had acquired the right-of-way to the beach close to Casmalia, and the community did not grow as other similar beach communities had in California. It was stuck in the past and had not prospered. To many, I'm sure, it was a blight, but to me, its historic background and its later life as the center of a 1920's oil field were wonderful.

In addition to its early 1900's post office and general store located in the same actual historical western building, Casmalia is also home to the Hitching Post Restaurant, started in 1946, with just a little barbecue pit built into the ground that was actually outside the restaurant building. Through the years, it has become a favorite of both local Central Coast patrons and celebrities. The Hitching Post II Restaurant in Buellton was featured in the 2004 movie "Sideways". So, the community had its pluses and minuses.

I will never forget my first Casmalia School home visit. My trip on this occasion points out the differences in living accommodations in this rural community and why it has been designated as a Title I school district to receive federal government assistance for low-income students. Many of the folks lived in old, respectable, and well-kept dwellings—not the best in the world, but cozy. But not all were so fortunate. Today's trip would be an education for me about why many students could not perform as well in school and what poverty was all about, as well as appreciating my own fortunate, smug middle-class upbringing. When I arrived at the designated address, it was identified by the sign lying in the mud in the front yard. The home consisted of a small, dilapidated trailer in the middle of the lot. I was shocked to see the hogs in the yard wallowing in the deep mud. It was beyond belief. I had never seen anything like this before. Had I been transported by some magic spell to Appalachia in the blink of an eye? I pushed open the rickety old front gate and balanced myself on the wobbly board, held up by blocks, leading across the hog mud and fecal matter that led to the door of the trailer that was now standing wide open. I was extremely careful in this maneuver, as the mud looked like it was over a foot deep and the odor was horrendous. Reaching the door safely, I knocked and called out, "Is anyone home? I am Mr. McCalip, one of the teachers from the school." The door was open, and the room was full up to about 3 or 4 feet with piles of unwashed clothing. If the room had furniture, it was buried in the litter. I could not believe that anyone could live like this. Eventually, I heard a squeaky voice return my second call with, "What in the hell do you want?" Such was life in Casmalia and my work, which, because of twists and turns of fate, would turn out to be my lifelong career in this small community. But it was at this moment that I actually knew about poverty and why I chose to work in Casmalia.

My youth growing up in the 50's on a country road next to Orcutt, a suburb of Santa Maria in the first of many housing tracts, had warm and fond memories. Both my mom and dad were hard workers. My dad worked his way up from foreman to a plant supervisor at the Santa Maria Valley's sugar plant. My mom worked in the lab at the same plant. Growing up in the 50's was a period of idyllic simplicity and certainty. My best friend from my childhood was Kenny O'Dell, who later moved to Nashville and became a successful songwriter who was also the best man in our marriage. Kenny and I can be away from each other for long periods, but in an instant, we can regain our joint sense of humor. We are connected in spirit, as true friends are.

By contrast, the 60's, however, was a time of challenge and change. The Vietnam War and the looming draft changed my life forever. In my last year in high school, our gym teachers started to get us all ready for war even before it started. Obstacle courses were built around the football field, and every morning we were required to run laps and go over the many obstacles. I am sure this saved many of my classmates from death. My mother kept preparing large breakfasts for me each morning, and then each morning I would heave them up on the football field. Large meals and 1st period PE did not go well together. Dicky Giovannachi, another good friend, would always stop to comfort me on the field as other students ran by. Dicky ended up helping me on another occasion. Dances at the infamous Santa Maria Veteran's Memorial building were known to be dangerous because of heavy drinking and fighting. Unfortunately, I ended up outside, in the back of the building, being beat up on the ground by several individuals. Dicky came by and pulled them all off me; he was just that kind of guy. So later, after he was drafted, it was a surprise to me when he was killed, but not a surprise when I learned he was helping others. This news made a great impression on me and made me turn myself from a mediocre student into a diligent one. I did not want to go to war. I studied harder from that point forward. So, the war helped push me through college. I loved history, and as a young child, I loved to read history books from cover to cover. That became my college major. A politically liberal college education during those years gave students a mission to help others.

My first inclination after graduation was to join the Peace Corps. I forwarded an application, and in no time, I was accepted, and they were forwarding my plane ticket. But my assignment was Tonga in the Pacific. Being trapped on a tropical island for several years without access to eligible girls did not appeal to me, so I cancelled out. Expecting the inevitable, I shaved my head and started to run and exercise in preparation for the draft. My sister, a school photographer, found another course of action for me at Casmalia School, a small-title school serving poor, disadvantaged students. It was perfect for me, as it satisfied my need to serve and was in the United States. After landing the job, I immediately fell in love with the poor students and enjoyed working with them. We had many happy days. In particular, I remember David and Debra Diaz twins, who were in the 2nd grade, and the large Meza family, who had a slew of children who attended Casmalia School when I started working in the early 1900 school building. It was old and rickety. The job fulfilled all my needs, and I felt I was making a contribution to our country.

Humor was one of my main teaching techniques because it had been successful with me when I was a student. Every few years, I would do what I would call the "lying and peeking around the door gag on the students." First, I would act like I had an emergency and had to leave the classroom, but first I would give them a lecture about how they needed to behave while I was out of the room. I would then briskly exit the room, and I would wait a few minutes around the corner. At first, they would all behave, and it would be quiet, but slowly the noise level would increase. When it was just right, I would lie on the floor and peek around the bottom corner of the door with just my head and hand visible. Slowly, the students would notice my head and finger pointing at them, and the class would burst into laughter. Unfortunately for the recess aides, after this maneuver, the kids were wound up, so I am sure they did not fully appreciate my humor, but it did put everyone, including the teachers' aides, in a good mood.

All new students to our school also had to put up with my "bb in my dimple joke". First, I would ask the new student if they noticed my large dimple on just one side of my face. I would then tell them about my unfortunate accident when I was a child with a BB gun and how I still had the BB lodged in my face. The whole class would become silent in anticipation of this story's climax. Then I would push out my tongue in my jaw, pushing with my finger, saying they were welcome to feel the BB. When they tried to touch my dimple, I would make a growling sound and snap at their finger. The whole class would burst into laughter, and they had completed their initiation to Casmalia School. Teaching at Casmalia School had fond memories when all was going smoothly.

During my years at Casmalia, I also tried to have the school make up for the bleak home existence for many of the students with the extra effort of the staff to supplement what was lacking at home because of poverty. They just did not do what middle-class families could afford to do with their families. The entire school puts on a massive holiday play each school year to entertain parents with participation from each and every student. In addition, each school year, we would rent a school bus and take field trips ranging from historical interest locations to Disneyland. It was a major undertaking, but both parents and staff pitched in. Science each year was made to come alive by constructing such items as solar ovens for each student to take home or the dissection of owl pellets and reassembly of the bones. Hands-on was the name of the game, and I loved teaching with the students. I loved hands-on projects and actually going and seeing items of interest. We went above and beyond what most schools provided. What better job could a teacher and principal have than being in charge of all these events?

Being in my early twenties, I dated several young women, including Santa Barbara County Superior Court Judge Marion Smith's daughter, Jane Smith. Jane and I were attending a garden wedding reception for another college friend when I met my future wife and soul mate. We were married within the year. The two of us had quite a large wedding since my new wife's parents owned a clothing store and knew many folks in Santa Maria at the time. It was a wedding with over 500 people at the reception, and Marion Hancock, Pernelle's parents' good friend and the name sake of the local hospital and Junior College, provided us with limousine service from the church to the reception at the Santa Maria Inn. For me, it was quite a stressful event and a memorable day for a young fellow from Old Town Orcutt. Pernelle Lyon McCalip, my new wife, soon after the wedding, transferred to Cal Poly to finish up her bachelor's degree as I worked at Casmalia. During that time, the principal at my school retired, and I was asked to take over as principal. After Pernelle's graduation, teaching jobs were scarce, so Pernelle taught for a year at a local Catholic school.

In my fifth year at Casmalia, we both quit our teaching jobs and headed to the Los Angeles area, so I could attend law school and Pernelle could work on a master's degree in the evenings. Within a short time at law school, large knots of arthritis developed on all of my fingers, which changed my already poor handwriting into chicken scratch. I finished law school in the top portion of my class, but the bar exam was another matter.

During the four-year law school program that I was enrolled in, I had the good fortune to work as a law clerk for Los Angeles Superior Court Judge Paul Egley, who was a no-nonsense judge of the highest integrity who handled all of the Southern California desegregation cases. He was an excellent role model for me in my formative years and set the example of what I expected from judges later in life and in confrontations at Casmalia. Arthritis was my uncontrollable fate, and, after several failed attempts at the bar exam, we returned to Santa Maria, our home town. Although I never practiced law, my law education and law clerking were extremely useful in my coming confrontations at Casmalia. Fate, in the form of arthritis, intervened in our plans, and the road back to Casmalia was smooth.

After a tax class in law school, I became intrigued by real estate. Even before leaving law school on weekends and vacation periods, my wife and I would travel to Santa Maria and purchase and upgrade rental properties. On our return to Santa Maria, Pernelle quickly found work in the Orcutt School District. Law School graduates could take the real estate broker's exam with no sales experience, so after passing, I opened a real estate office that quickly grew to six sales associates.

My office did well as it was located on busy Clark Avenue in Old Town Orcutt. I started my new business at a time when retired people were selling and cashing out their homes in the crowded Los Angeles areas and moving to coastal California seeking better retirement living. They could afford a nice home for cash in Santa Maria with funds left over from the sale of their Southern California home. It was a perfect time to be in the real estate business. My small office was the first real estate office they would bump into after they pulled off the busy 101 freeway on the west-bound Clark exit. So almost every Sunday, I would have one or two prospective buyers to work with. I was at a point where I needed help.

That's when one day my soon-to-be good friend and associate arrived at my front office door. Alex Mayne, who had recently arrived from Australia, came bounding into the room. There, he had sold real estate and insurance. Australia was different than California in the sale of real estate because an attorney, after the agent found the home for the buyer, would do all the legal paperwork and also act as an escrow agent. So, the two of us were a perfect match, as he did not like to do the needed California contracts, and I, being fresh out of law school, could whack out those contracts with ease and in no time. He had a wonderful Aussie accent that proved to be hypnotic to buyers. I could tell that folks loved to listen to him talk, and I was always amazed at the buyers that he left with, who did not seem to be good prospects, who came back all smiles, ready for me to do the paperwork. We prospered in our new relationship.

Later, Alex and I got into flipping distressed properties before the term was even used or popular. He and I would work on slow days refurbishing homes, and I will never forget the two of us using just a compressor and paint buckets with a homemade nozzle to paint the exterior of one of the homes. It worked brilliantly, but the two of us ended up covered in paint! Later, we acquired a paint sprayer. Eventually, my small office expanded to six sales agents, and this kept me hopping. Luckily, most agents were out in the field most of the time because it was difficult for all of us to fit within the confines of the small office.

I enjoyed my years in this real estate activity, but one day Harold Wollam from Casmalia came into the office and announced to me that the Board of Trustees at Casmalia would like me to come back to work as the Superintendent/Principal. I answered that I was flattered that they wanted me back, but that I would have to discuss it with my wife first. I would get back to him the following day.

Harold Wollam was an elderly gentleman married to the school matriarch, Winifred Wollam, for whom the school was eventually named. She had been on the board when I first went to work at Casmalia after I had finished college. She and Harold had known my dad when he lived in Casmalia briefly after his post-depression arrival in California. This relationship had helped me land my first job in this small district my first time around.

We wanted to start a family, so we accepted the offer. I considered the principal position as an easy, no-stress job with health insurance, which we needed to start our family. My assessment of stress changed after a few years and the future confrontations. Thus, I kept running my real estate office and worked at the school; being young, the long hours worked out great. Life seemed fine both at school and at the office.

Later, after the birth of our son, John, this schedule became too hectic, and I sold the office to an associate.

FIRST "CANARY IN THE MINE SHAFT"

It was also at this time in our busy lives that a major economic setback occurred. Pernelle was low person on the totem pole at the neighboring Orcutt School District and thus when funds became low, she was reluctantly let go. What then appeared to be good fortune turned incredibly bad in hindsight. I happened to have need of a teacher at our school so she started out working with me. After working for a portion of the year she was asked to return to Orcutt. It was at this time that we were attempting to have our first child who was to be named Kelly after we joyfully found out her sex. But this joy turned to sadness when Pernelle noticed no kicking for several days and a trip to the doctor confirmed her death. The still birth was a shocker to us both and brought many tears from Pernelle, but I maintained my stoic nature trying to be upbeat around Pernelle and her mother, but when alone my tears also flowed. This event should have alerted me to the danger of living and working in Casmalia, but it was far in advance of the cumulative effect of events to come.

The birth of our son, John, and later, our daughter, Meghan, refocused our personal lives. I was taken aback by the fact that fathers were now expected to attend the birth of children, which was unlike my father, who went fishing with my sister when I was born. Birthing classes took up much time for the both of us, but it was worth the effort when I saw John's wide eyes looking at me and the world around him immediately at birth, as if to say, Where, in the heck am I and what is this place? Meghan's entrance into the world was quite different, as she was squinting at me and making a lot of noise, crying until she was held. Our personal lives were now complete with the birth of the two of them. We had been truly blessed with healthy, happy children.

But after pondering this chain of life events and my background, I needed to plan a course of action. It was clear to me as I sat behind my desk, after my physical confrontation, that I could not abandon my students and the community at a time of need. It was also clear to me that something deep inside me did not like to be pushed around; it was my nature to push back and to keep moving forward. So, whoever was in the way—the dump owner, the county, the state, or the federal government—should all look out because, from this day forward, I planned to be active and hit them hard. It was now time to play hardball!

CHAPTER 4

FRIENDS AND FOES

CAP GROUP FORMED—CASMALIANS AGAINST POLLUTION

From the time of my physical confrontation, I wanted to take a more active and aggressive role in the effort to close and cap the toxic waste site, Casmalia Resources. So, during the following week I called several community members and families to get the ball rolling.

First, on my list was Kenneth Vaniter and his wife Phyllis. Ken, was a tall, distinguished, even tempered retired older gentleman, who had many grown family members with their own families living in the community. His quiet well thought out counsel proved invaluable in the years that lay ahead. He became my close ally who I could always count upon during the next few years.

Next, I phoned Nick Irmiter and his wife Angie, who worked at the local hospital. Both had recently moved into the area from out of state. Nick was a handsome young man, with a slow western drawl who had worked in the oil fields prior to their move to California. He looked and talked as if he were straight out of a western movie. Nick was looking to upgrade his employment status in California and thus had time to pitch in on our efforts. He was the father of two beautiful young daughters who attend Casmalia School.

Third on the list was Jerry Corlew and his wife Cynthia, another young man, who worked at home making and selling fishing lures. He and his wife had a young pre-school child. Jerry needed the low rent that Casmalia afforded to keep his fishing lure business afloat. All three community members I contacted that day were in essence trapped in Casmalia either because of the need to continue to have low rents or because of an inability to sell their property because of the closeness of the dump site. They all three also had free time to devote to our joint efforts.

Nick and Jerry became the community contacts for Greenpeace, a welcome ally. When a large group was in town they stayed in Nick and Jerry's homes. Greenpeace led by Bradly Angel from San Francisco, was just the group to give the community that spark and that fighting spirit. Bradly was an aggressive young man who was the field director for Greenpeace and who had participated efforts to protect whales in our oceans. But, at first, I was quietly leery of Greenpeace as their worldwide reputation had preceded them. Greenpeace was fighting for environmental causes in every corner of the world. I had read of their exploits in Scotland protesting the dumping of toxics in the ocean, off the coast of California protecting whales, and on the high seas protesting seal clubbing as well as nuclear weapons testing. They were known to stop at nothing including illegal activities to achieve their goals. Later in the struggle I was moved to tears by the sacrifices of community members, both young and old, inspired by this group who were not afraid of arrest and imprisonment for our environmental cause. I was amazed at how many community members followed their example and footsteps to jail!

Nick, Jerry and Ken were sitting in the principal's office waiting for me to complete my duties teaching in my classroom. The new office was adorned in photos of past presidents that I had hoped would inspire students to learn about a few of the more recent ones. The office was small but had an interior window that allowed viewing into the adjacent classroom, which was handy if I had to take calls in my position as principal/superintendent. My job was hectic during normal years but we were about to embark upon an even more demanding activity of open warfare with the dump site.

I slid down into the principal's chair as they told me the new name of the group: CAP or Casmalians Against Pollution. I quickly responded that that sounded like a great name and expounded our ultimate goal of capping the site and they could count me in. It was in this first contact, having not yet evolved into an environmental activist, with Jerry, Ken and Nick after the school closure that I laid down the rules for my involvement, From the expressions on their faces I could tell they were a bit taken back by my comments. I had teaching and administrative certificates to protect and it was explained to everyone that I could not be involved in the "planning of or participation in any illegal activities. Please leave me out of the loop on these activities." With Greenpeace I knew this was a strong possibility. I further explained that I had already received a threatening letter from the dump owner's attorney telling me personally to shut up or be sued. So I was sure I would become their main target. I

assured everyone that I would become very outspoken. The entire explanation seemed to relive the anxious expressions. Only later would I realize how much of a main target I would become!

Nineteen Eighty-Five became quite a year for our efforts, with both successes and setbacks. In addition to Greenpeace many new allies stepped forward to help out. Early in the year Meg, the school secretary, interrupted me in class for an important phone call. It was an out of state east coast medical doctor who has seen reports on the national media of our situation. He was familiar with cyanide exposures and strongly felt that we had all been exposed to cyanide gas. He quickly gave me a history lesson about toxics slowly evolving in industrial plants in Switzerland and Germany and moving to Americas' east cost in New Jersey. He told me about how dangerous cyanide was and how Zyklon B, the cyanide-based poison gas had been used in the Nazi death camps. Being my usual skeptical self, I cut the call short as I had to get back to my class. After thanking him for the call, on the way back to the classroom, I thought to myself that he must be a possible nut case. How could he have ascertained this from just a TV description of our lack of oxygen? There were so many toxins in the air who could possibly tell. Years later, I discovered, this turned out to be advice I should have listen too much closer.

It was also at this time that 76 local doctors signed on against Casmalia Resources as a Public health hazard citing a rise in the entire Santa Maria Valley of various illness and still births. Dr. Steve Williams testified before the county supervisors about health abnormalities and that continued exposures could result in leukemia and other long term health issues. His request from his group of doctors was for an immediate emergency closure of the site.

Unfortunately, Dr. Williams' home and office were later vandalized. This was becoming a hot button issue as large sums of money, jobs, and influence were at stake. The community appreciated Dr. Williams putting himself on the line and the group of doctors' strong support, but the effort did not get the needed support of a majority of the board of supervisors. From the outset only one county supervisor, 5th District Supervisor Toru Miyoshi, was consistent in strongly supporting our small community's efforts. On the other hand, 4th District Supervisor DeWayne Holmdahl, in whose district the community sat, consistently voted against us and became a dump spokesperson. He and his aide tried to convince us and the general public that the fumes were nothing more than one of the waste ponds turning "septic". His laughable solution was "Perhaps some oil sprayed on top would help stop the problem".

Local environmental activists also started to come forward to help us. Kathie Hoxie, an attractive young woman who was active in local

Santa Barbara County politics, became a strong and helpful ally who helped with major community events both at the school site and later in Sacramento at the governor's office. Joyce Howerton, the future mayor of the neighboring city of Lompoc, and Ilene Pickle all gave us strong support in planning many events. Hugh Hanna from Santa Barbara, with a strong technical background and who had served on the grand jury, later joined the effort, after his term expired. As time went on, I began to be referred to as an environmental activist as well as a school principal. My later confrontations and experiences made me proud of the new title.

I was becoming increasingly aware of the strength of opponents of our small poor community of 300 men, women, and children whom we now faced in local, state, and national industry coupled with politics at every level. The influence and sway they had over public health officials at all levels of government was monumental and appeared overwhelming. Locally the owners of the facility were a Who's Who of the local Santa Maria Valley and Santa Barbara oil with financial interests with Kenneth Hunter from the wealthy area of Montecito close to Santa Barbara, as the managing partner. The major partners, according to the Santa Barbara News and Review on October 17, 1985, consisted of Kenneth Hunter, 25 percent general partner interest plus a 6.6 percent interest in the limited partnership, Mario and George V. Castagnola 32.6 percent interest, Bruce Edward Conway 20 percent interest, Pozo Casmalia 13.32 percent interest. Miles Sharkey refused to comment about his interest, and Carl Engle and Joe Gray of Santa Maria would only say, "none of your business".

NO REST FOR THE WICKED

No sooner than we had the school up and running again, in December, two financial problems popped up. The first problem was from the dump site's lackey and county health director, Dr. Hart, who luckily swayed in the wind with public opinion. Dr. Hart and I started a series of phone calls and letters dealing with who should pay for the costs of the health care nurse assigned to our district. Should it be our school district or the county health department? He contended to us that his department did not have the appropriate budget to handle the expense and he would have to look to the school district for reimbursement. I countered to him that the need for the nurse was because of a major public health issue that went far beyond

our school district boundaries caused by a failure of the county public health department to fulfill its duties to protect the public in the area in general. Thus, the cost should be the county's. Coming events overshadowed this dispute and the county ended up paying this expense.

The second financial problem that the district now faced was declining enrollment. Because of the emergency closure and the community crisis, our enrollment dropped from above 30 students in our small school to about 20. Those families who did not own their home or had other resources understandably moved to safer locations. In California, school districts get funding from the state based on enrollment. I needed all seven full time and part time employees to efficiently run the school. Bill Cirone, the County Superintendent of schools, who came from the East Coast and had a wonderful accent that set him apart from other Californians, came to our rescue. After a brief phone conversation, he informed me that emergency funding was available to schools that were impacted by emergencies such as ours, but it required the state legislature to pass a special law for just our district. He and his business department went to work immediately on this problem. This he succeeded in doing and our original 30 student funding continued through the long duration of this community crisis.

ALLIES IN THE NEWS MEDIA

Casmalia Resources had a sophisticated full time public relations director, Jan Lachenmaier, who thank goodness for our community did a so-so job, but not an outstanding job. As time went on and we became more proficient in the art of public relations we hammered away at her main themes. The main public relation message she espoused was that the toxic dump business was a, "state of the art operation". To say the least the art was pretty primitive. She would frequently boast about the health of employees, that our private investigators later found was untrue from interviews with former employees. She had an uphill battle because, the illegal toxic overflows into the watershed, the toxic materials migrating underground off site from unlined lagoons, and the growing public awareness of hazardous of enhanced evaporation techniques being used at the site were untested and unsafe.

Against this full time, experienced public relations director, with unlimited funds, a group of public relations novices began their efforts. The news media flocked to the school after the emergency closure. The initial TV and newspaper interviews were conducted on a one-on-one basis, which turned out to be the way to proceed in the future. This worked well in the first few months. I would always send them down the street to the community after they came to me for the school district's view point, and to talk to Nick Irmiter, Kenneth Vaniter or Jerry Corlew to get the rest of the community's view point. But it soon became apparent that this would need to be a long-term effort so I consulted an old buddy, Richard Garcia, from high school days who was the director of news at a local TV station. After talking with him it became apparent that we needed to have a new story each week or every few days to get the reporters to the school and community. So, after this meeting we started the dribble policy; we would not tell all the facts we had about a news-worthy event. We would dribble small bits out.

My old buddy assured me at the end of our conversation that he would send a crew out whenever I needed one. Friends are a great asset and I will always be indebted.

Next, I was invited to attend a news conference at one of the Los Angeles toxic dump sites

It certainly was a learning event for me. It was easy to do a one-on-one-interviews with a TV newscaster because you could talk to one person and you knew who to look at, but when I arrived, there was a line of cameras set up from six or seven or more stations. I muddled my way through this event because I was befuddled as to who I was talking with and who and where to focus my attention and vision. From that point forward, I always tried to talk to one station at a time for a more natural interview even if several stations showed up. After six years we became experts at one-on-one-interviews as well as public relations.

NOTORITY AND TARGET DAY

With the notoriety I was getting as one of the spokespersons for the community, it did not dawn on me that there were people with a vested and serious interest in stopping me by any means. Some of those folks consisted of employees of the toxic dump site. It was their livelihood that kept each dump employee's family household together. The intensity of their dislike for what I had come to represent motivated the afternoon events of this otherwise normal day.

It had been a good day with no odors or events and I left a little late on this afternoon from the school waving at students playing along the road in front of the post office and general store, located in the old western building. The students were all smiles as I passed by.

My personal safety was the farthest thought in my mind as I turned and started down the winding country road through the foothills past NTU road and turned on to State Highway One. My radio was blaring with country music as I went merrily on my way home to my beautiful new wife. I rarely saw another car on these roads as it was far out in the county, but then I noticed a large pick-up truck speeding up behind me. The driver got uncomfortably close to my rear bumper which was strange because I always traveled on this road at a fairly high rate of speed because no one else was usually on the road. He then quickly darted out to pass me but cut in before going around driving me off the road.

My car spun out off the road, out of control, narrowly missing a fence post and power pole. My anger emerged again and I became enraged instantly and pulled back on to the roadway putting my gas pedal to the floor and in a flash was behind the idiot. Returning the favor, I was now just a few feet from his rear bumper. His speed increased as he tried to get away. We were both now traveling at super high speeds. As we reached the turn off to Old Town Orcutt, I started to regain my composure and sanity and slowed down for the turn as he continued on down Highway One. I hoped whoever he was he learned that I would not put up with this behavior. Only later did I recognize this young man as a dump employee. He testified at one of many of the hearings about how good his health was working at a toxic dump. At this later hearing seeing him as a dump employee I became concerned about my own families' safety as I took into account the earlier vandalism to Dr. Williams' home and office.

LAW FIRMS

The community at this time had started seeking legal representation to sue the dump site owner. Some community members signed up with local attorney Richard Brenneman and others signed up with attorney Cory Birnberg from San Francisco. I tried to work with both law offices when called upon. Through the six years the communities legal representation changed to different law firms. Cory eventually transferred his interest to Robert Sulnick, a Loyola Law Professor. Later a larger firm from Los Angeles , the Toxey Hall Smith firm, was added to the mix. Later on an even financially stronger firm also joined our ranks.

The school district remained with the county counsel's office that represented the entire county of Santa Barbara. This representation did not work for us during our time of crisis, with apparent conflicts of interest and the sharing of information with the dump owner, so I started asking tough questions concerning their ability to represent us starting in December of 1984 and their opinion as to us getting private legal representation. It took until May of 1985 and many letters to finally get a clear answer. By letter, the county counsel's office finally notified me that they could represent us in matters involving the waste disposal facility only if our position was not contrary to the interest of the County of Santa Barbara. The California Education Code does authorize the district to engage outside legal services, so we were now free to work directly with private law firms along with the community. Separate private law firms became imperative later when the county became a defendant and liable because of negligent regulatory oversight. These private law firms became our strongest and most important allies. Eventually the firms filled lawsuits totaling over one billion, for the community of Casmalia, against the site and this certainly added to the eventual growing pressure on the toxic dump site to close. Closure was a long way down a treacherous and dangerous road that lay ahead for the community, but our hodgepodge group moved boldly forward!

CHAPTER 5

SCHISM

STATE AND COUNTY AIR TESTING

Much like my office confrontation and task force meeting, nineteen eighty-five turned into a year of irritation for the community with the air pollution inspector, who was assigned the task of inspecting the dump site and responding to complaints of fumes and odors. This sorry chap was Jon Carroll, who espoused the county line that was uniform from the top, Dr. Hart, the director, to the bottom, pathetic inspector Carroll. The first response to a complaint was that they could not smell the odors. If they could, there was no "scientific" way of knowing where they were coming from. This was so absurd that it was comical. The reeking dump site was only a little more than a mile away from the complaint he was responding to at the time, and community members had on occasion walked up to the site. Only a fool would assert such hogwash. It was clear to the community that the state and county health departments did not have their best interests in mind and, in fact, were protecting the interests of big oil and toxic waste industries. Jon Carroll, we later found through an investigator, did not even look at the Zimpro Unit's log when he casually drove past the unit as it sprayed toxic steam into the air. Thus, the county had, early on, continually poisoned its relationship with the community.

It was with this bad community feeling that air testing was set to begin in June of 1985. It was apparent to the community that all of the nine sprinkler pipe spray areas used to dispose of toxic waste into the air had been turned off at the beginning of May. Thus, the board of trustees requested that I prepare a "business as usual" board resolution and cover letter from me to the County Counsel requesting that the Zimpro Processing Machine and Evaporation Systems be up and running during any air testing. It was our feeling that any air testing under these current closed conditions would be useless. The response was not timely or helpful, so the district has now started using the private law firms used by the community. Again, I prepared a resolution authorizing attorney Cory Birnberg to contact the state health department with the district's request.

In essence, we requested that the dump site owner not be allowed to establish the testing protocol, as he was now doing, as it would prove nothing and business as usual should be followed. In addition, the community should be involved in establishing the protocol. It was also pointed out that students would be gone for the summer months, and it was thus a perfect time for testing to be done correctly. Unfortunately, despite our best efforts, testing was done in the dump's shutdown mode. This further alienated the community from the state and county health departments.

The Board of Supervisors' meeting to discuss the agenda item and our request was held in far-off, sunny Santa Barbara, far away from any angry community members. It was a typical board meeting to debate the disputed item. Good old Dr. Hart took the lead at the meeting and argued against our community and school district requests for all spray systems and equipment to be on prior to air testing and during the actual testing. The county Board of Supervisors decided not to insist that the spray systems be on. And why not? This decision was made on the advice of the county's top health official, who said the dump site had told the state they would not resume spraying again. At this point, I should have tried to sell the board a "bucket of sand," as Dr. Hart and the dump's position was outlandish considering the dump owner's obsession with taking in more waste. Supervisor Miyoshi was the only one who spoke up and stated, "I sense they (Casmalia Resources) are merely trying to reduce operations during the testing period". In response, our adversary, Supervisor DeWayne Holmdahl, figured that if the firm was to stop A spraying, "then the air testing without it would reflect reality". Miyoshi argued that "the point is not to duplicate conditions, but to keep their operations at status quo during the testing". Hart was still sticking to his old story that there was no way to tell the source of the odors without scientific testing. He argued that insisting that all systems be on would only hold up the testing program that needed to get started. The first phase would see if any toxins were in the air, and the second phase would pinpoint the source. This argument and plan later became laughable when the number of angry calls escalated and Hart had his staff use their noses to pinpoint the source. However, he succeeded with the board, and all systems were off. We later found he, his department, and the county had much poor conduct to hide from the public. It was another of many confrontations, some won and some lost. On this day, we lost!

It was at this time that the community got word from its attorneys of the results of four randomly selected children's blood and health testing at Children's Hospital in Oakland, California. It was not normal. The hospital noted some patterns of concern in all four children that may be present in all of the Casmalia population if these four children were typical. The results showed depressed white blood cell counts and immune systems, liver, and kidney damage. All these readings are common with toxic exposures around toxic factories and dumps. The testing showed the community the seriousness of our plight!

On September 28, Attorney Robert Sulnick contacted all the clients, reminding them that the County of Santa Barbara had vested interest in keeping the dump site open and that they should refer any request for health information to his office and that any testing should be "done by our physicians with your best interest in mind. Please tell the county that your participation is conditioned upon your attorney's approval."

HEALTH SURVEY AND TESTING

Jan Schienly, a Professor of Health Science at California State University Northridge, started working for our attorneys in November of 1985. She was responsible for collecting and coordinating all health information. She was a professional who was immediately liked and loved by the entire community. Unfortunately, she became a target of the County Health Department, just as I had become a target of employees at the dump site.

Out of the 67 local doctors from Santa Maria who supported us, Drs. Ducoffe, Williams, Okerblom, and Haque provided medical testing for the community. Ken Vaniter helped make appointments. It was truly a community effort and a major undertaking. But by 1986, the vindictive leader of the County Health Department and someone in his department had made arrangements to try to get Jan fired from her position at Northridge University and removed from the doctorate program. I could again feel my blood boiling, but I managed a controlled response. This set off a barrage of letters from me and Santa Maria doctors, as well as state legislators. After laying out the county's disgusting behavior in a dignified manner in my letter, I went on to say:

"It is easy for me to recommend for continued employment with your department, Jan Schienle, who stepped into this politically chaotic situation and brought order where none existed, brought professionalism where public health care was scorned, but most importantly, through her warm and friendly manner, brought peace of mind to a troubled community.

In particular, Jan was able to organize and gain the respect of 67 local Santa Maria physicians; set up and run a blood and urine testing clinic here at our school; canvass door-to-door for a detailed health questionnaire she prepared; plan, organize, and transport an entire community for physical exams; make contact and do the same activities in a nearby community for a control group. She is now in the process of bringing this data together.

It appears that Jan's work will set the standard for years to come in the area of toxic exposure. It is important that your university's name be in eluded in this important work.

With this information in mind, I can attest to the fact that Jan has completed substantial work toward the completion of her doctorate degree in a professional manner. It would be a disservice to your university and to health care in this state to not let her continue."

It was my hope that this letter helped her out after she was targeted by our disgruntled local health department.

Jan's initial list of injuries and health issues found in the health survey, just to name a few, consisted of the following information:

50% of the town folks were suffering from long-term chronic bronchitis or upper chronic respiratory problems during the prior year.

65% became ill after exposure to fumes, and of these, 73% complained of headaches, 58% of nausea, and 56% of eye irritation.

10 persons developed high blood pressure after exposure. (Two individuals after acute exposure had instant high blood pressure.)

The death toll was high during the past few years for the 200 people surveyed. 1980–1985 (total of 10 deaths consisting of 1 leukemia, 3 lung cancers, 3 burst vessels in the lungs, and 3 stillbirths)

It was at this time that the new legal team suggested that the district prepare a disclosure form and statement for parents to sign, which indicated the distance to the dump and that numerous harmful toxins had been found in air samples, and that we might be required to close under emergency conditions and also to provide a second home for the student to be sent to if the parent was not available on emergency closure.

ALL CALIFORNIA TOXIC DUMPS LEAKING

The dump owner's public relations director touted the fact that there was no water under the Casmalia site, despite numerous ranch wells in the area, and that the ground at the site was impermeable, and was thus safe to use unlined lagoons. In 1985 a coalition of environmental groups released a report on the five Class I Toxic Dumps in California including the Casmalia Dump Site. It reported, "The extremely hazardous waste seeps through ground that had been considered geologically impermeable based on examination of state and federal documents". The report was titled "No Where to Go". Concern over leakage grew in California after leakage at the Stringfellow Dump site and acid pits near Riverside, "Toxic contaminants, including acids, heavy metals and pesticides, leaked endangering drinking supplies for half a million people in Southern California. Federal Super fund money was used to clean it up and transport waste to Casmalia and other sites." The report predicted, "a bleak and toxic game of leapfrog from one dump to another. Thus, there is no Class I site presently operating in California that meets even the paper definition of safe containment." Unfortunately, the State Health Department was forced to deal with problems in highly populated areas by moving waste to Casmalia with a small meager poor population of 200 to 300 souls without political clout and to protect large Los Angeles industries and political donors.

After this disclosure of information our school district also decided to conduct our own test of water wells and surface water in the area of the school and community through a certified direct mail company. This was to be the same water that the state, county, and the dump site owner said did not exist.

AIR TESTING AND CORRELATION WITH TOXIC PONDS

I eventually became so frustrated with the county's continuing comical assertion that they could not locate the source of odors and fumes that I shot off a letter to the Santa Barbara County Grand Jury. It read in part:

"During the first few months of 1985, after the November 1984 closure of our school I, on numerous occasions, asked for copies of pond reports, 12/5/84 and 12/28/84 from both Mr. Steve Lavinger (SDHS) and Mr. Jon Carroll (SBAPCD).

Mr. Lavinger stated initially that they would be forthcoming, but later stated that they formed the basis of an Administrative Complaint against Hunter Resources and would be released only after this was settled.

During the first few months of 1985 I spoke to Mr. Jon Carroll on the phone and he stated that the county (he and Mr. Fredricks) had possession of courtesy copies. He then gave me details of raw findings. In particular 7 of the 11 toxins identified in the Radion Air Study were found in aeration ponds at the site. During the conversation he read from the report he had in front of him. However, after consulting with Fredricks, his superior, he refused to give me copies.

During this time period the official county position was that they could not determine the source of odors. This is a difficult position to maintain if you have an air report and a corresponding pond reports in your possession.

We again made efforts to obtain copies of these reports. Mrs. Tammy Royce, who is gathering information for us states that Mr. Fredricks cannot locate these. She is now requesting copies from the state. Two years is long enough to wait. I would appreciate you obtaining these documents by issuing subpoenas for these from both the state and county."

The letter did not result in copies of the reports, but it did result in the Grand Jury eventually calling for the closure of the site as a real and present danger to public health in a later grand jury report. It also, I am sure, caused some grief for reluctant air pollution control employees who I am sure were called to appear before the grand jury. The divide between the local do- nothing regulators and the community continued to grow in anger and intensity as future events unfolded.

PART TWO: LET THE BATTLE BEGIN

CHAPTER 6

BACKPEDALING (GREENPEACE, WIND CHANGE, AND MORE TRUCKS)

TRUCKS START TO CLOG LOCAL ROADS

Truck traffic at Casmalia Resources could turn the front gate and NTU road into a parking lot on most days with large toxic haulers backed up as far as the eye can see. In addition to the existing truck traffic clogging county roads, in February of 1985 Hunter started serious negotiations with the State Health Department about accepting the McColl waste from Los Angeles County. The issue of negotiations was $13.50 per ton or $140.00 per ton to be paid for by Federal Super Fund money. Under the state plan the McColl's waste would be relocated to Casmalia because of the threat they posed to neighboring residences around the McColl site. An estimated 130,000 tons will be transported or roughly $18,000,000 for Casmalia Resources. This will add 40 trucks per day coming from Fullerton California which will be added to the existing truck traffic lined up at the gate on NTU Road. Total cost of the McColl clean-up was estimated at $28,000,000. Again, during these negotiations I am sure Mr. Hunter's eyes were aglow with dollar signs.

Hunter and his site manager, James McBride, at this point started a public relations offensive to sell the site to the public with a theme that the site was, "Not the problem, but part of the solution to waste disposal." They mentioned also the old theme that it was a, "State of the Art Operation". They then touted many of their supposed great methods. The offensive contained many omitted and misleading statements made by Mr. McBride and Mr. Hunter. First, they contended that the Zimpro Wet Air Oxidation system was being operated with a permit since it was installed. It was found later that no permanent permit was ever issued by the county and there was virtually no county supervision by the air pollution control district, with massive overruns of the system. Out of unlined lagoons the site used farming spray systems to enhanced evaporation. None of these items could be called state of the art or proven methods. In fact, these systems had filled all the surrounding valleys, and our school facility, with toxic fumes. Other claims made by the two insisted that all employees were always in good health. This was later found not to be true by the community's private investigators. Two workers hit by enhanced evaporation spray while working at the site ended up with white spots on the skin, bloody noses for five days and blood abnormalities.

At this same time on February 14, 1985 Supervisor DeWayne Homedahl came out as usual in support of the dump site by claiming that the source of fumes had not been identified, which reaffirmed his faith that Casmalia Resources was a safe operation. It could be fairly stated by this time that the community of Casmalia had developed an understandable hatred of this particular county supervisor.

It was also at this time that a reporter from Time Magazine arrived at my office door wanting to do a story about the school closure and the town's problems. He was working on a national story about toxics and wanted to feature us as one of the communities impacted. After talking to him I sent him down to interview others in the community. It would be a month or so before his article would appear, but it gave the community excellent national exposure. We were also starting to get good exposure in the Los Angeles Times. All this helped us get leverage with local and state leaders.

GREENPEACE ARRIVES

Truck traffic had started to increase and was up to 130 per day from 60 because of the clean-up in Southern California and was really clogging county roads by the time Greenpeace arrived. Greenpeace was famous for protecting the whales from extinction in the Pacific using whatever means it took and I was admittedly apprehensive about their arrival in Casmalia, but Bradley Angel, the leader, proved to be a dedicated person, an outstanding example for the community to follow. The community needed that spark of resistance and Greenpeace showed them how.

As originally planned the Greenpeace group stayed in the homes of Jerry and Nick as well as other town folks and plans were made for the first of many community protests at the gate to the facility to be instigated on August 12, 1985. About 200 angry protesters arrived and I diligently called all the media outlets to make sure it got plenty of coverage. Eleven protesters chained themselves to the main gate blocking all truck traffic. All eleven were arrested including Jerry and two other local folks. It got plenty of press coverage. Just what we needed!

WIND AND CLIMATE CHANGE

September 1985 brought a change of fate for the small community of Casmalia with a change of wind direction and local climate. Fumes that had piled up in all the small valleys in the Orcutt foothills similar to the one in which Casmalia sat, suddenly blew down into the adjacent Santa Maria Valley and in particular, the highly populated Orcutt area. Calls started to flood the Air Pollutions Control District which was a sub-agency of the County Health Department. Over 200 calls in one day from the public and from the large Orcutt Union School District who had logged in 220 complaints from students with eye and runny nose complaints. It was a sweet pungent chemical odor which was the same as in Casmalia. Ten days later the same type of event occurred again. Dr. Jack Garvin, the superintendent at the Orcutt District, was not the type to take any guff from the health department. He and his district made plans with State Senator Art Torres for a State Senate hearing at the Orcutt School District.

Dr. Hart suddenly saw the light and was able to send out five inspectors who used their noses to trace the smell to the toxic dump. He was now able to say that the dump was the source. Amazing how Dr. Hart could bend in the wind when the complaints swelled. He could, now under public pressure, disregard his earlier insistence on a more scientific approach that he just could not fund earlier with his department. Casmalia Resources and Dr. Hart made quick efforts to cover the ponds with foam to cut down on odors. Despite the fact it helped the community's position, my dislike for this man grew with each passing day and each changing position

Dr. Hart was still bugging me and the district by letter for payment for the cost of the public health nurse; a letter I refused to even answer. He was certainly not skilled at public relations. If he wanted the money, he would have to take me to small claims court. This would have been great publicity for the district and our efforts to close the dump site. I am sure I could have filled the court complex with news media; our small district against the county that was making about three million in taxes a year from dump operations. He did not bite and eventually I heard no more on this subject as events slowly changed in our favor.

MORE TRUCKS AND PUBLIC IRRITATION

With the closing of the Southern Dump sites in the state, the number of trucks on the road in Santa Barbara County had increased substantially as did hazardous waste spills. From 1984 through 1986 there were nine hazardous material spills in the South Coast region along the highways, including one in May of 1984 that forced evacuations in Santa Barbara near Highway 101. In 1984 a lot of the vehicles were purchased second hand and were used oil field vehicles and many were not even designed to transport hazardous waste, but as the Southern California Dumps closed, they were used for hazardous waste transport to cash in on the gold rush for some of that government super fund money that could be made in transport. Depending on the route they could go through Santa Barbara, Los Alamos, Orcutt or Santa Maria. These routes and news of spills outraged the public in each of these areas. The outrage brought needed support to our efforts!

To put a stop to the public outcry caused by spills and transport through populated areas the California Highway Patrol, to their credit the most responsive state agency, started to make surprise inspections of trucks hauling hazardous waste. Surprise inspections were set up at different locations but frequently about two miles south of Los Alamos on Highway 101. Inspectors were often at the location from 4:30 AM until noon. Log books, licenses, medical cards and manifests for the load were all looked at. Inspectors dressed in protective clothing took samples of the hazardous liquids to check against the manifests. Frequently, loads that listed 98 percent water and 2 percent toxic materials were reversed. Flammability, acidity and alkalinity were all checked on the spot. It was these inspections that helped cut down on traffic to the dump and helped it become safer. It was much needed because the dump site did what they called a "thump test" to make sure something was in the container. No actual inspections were conducted by the dump site we later found out from investigators for the community. Nothing seemed to surprise me any longer, but it was Dr. Hart, the county health director's, transformation and change of position under public pressure that was boggling to behold!

CHAPTER 7

STATE SENATE HEARING AND LARGER PROTEST

STATE SENATE HEARING

Impacting large areas of the county certainly gets immediate attention as State Senator Art Torres, Chairman of the Senate Toxics and Public Safety Committee, calls for his committee to meet at the Orcutt School District on Oct. 9, 1985 to gather information and to call for a dump "501 Closure Hearing" by the State Health Department. John Ramey, chief deputy director of the State Health Department stated at the beginning of the hearing that a 501 Closure Hearing is, "… not warranted at this time". After this announcement Torres said," he would be contacting the governor and urged other Senators and panel members to do the same." Torres went on to say, "Anytime children are made ill by toxic waste and schools are forced to close it is a tragedy. When state, federal and local agencies responsible for the protection of the public health fail to act, it is a scandal."

David Roe, representing the Environmental Defense Fund, opened public testimony by claiming, "The question before the committee is whether or not Casmalia Resources is safe? The only thing that the State Department of Health Services and the Regional Water Quality

Control Board know is that they don't know. Preliminary indication from studies of water wells around the dump indicate there is trouble. Alarms have been ringing, ringing, ringing since November of 1984 yet none of the responsible agencies have ever visited the dump to determine what's setting off the alarm."

Numerous people spoke and finally Jack Garvin, Superintendent of Orcutt School District. His message was, " that out of his 3,000 students, 20% or 600 complained of symptoms including runny noses and eyes, sore throats and nausea." He described the side effects as, "continual dosing of children by toxics". My comments were described as equally succinct as Jack's comments, "Close it, cap it and clean it up." I further added, "that Casmalia area residents had complained for a long time about the same problems believing they were linked to the dump, but the results we got were zilch. Because of this response from local and state health officials, I think the community should seriously consider vacating the area ". I then made a pitch for the peaceful demonstration scheduled for Oct. 26th to be held at NTU and Black roads. This ended up being free advertising for the event on all media outlets. The turnout on the 26th was beyond our wildest dreams!

Our strong supporter, Supervisor Toru Miyoshi said," the facility did about $4 million worth of business in July alone. The Casmalia toxic dump is out of control". He added that, "...until it is proved to be no threat to the health and safety of local residents it should be closed." Miyoshi labeled the failures of all toxic dumps in the country as, "low -tech answers to high -tech problems." Our local supervisor DeWayne Holmdahl, was nowhere to be found at the hearing, as I am sure, he knew that his usual comments in support of the dump would bring rousing boos from the assembled group.

Hunter described the hearing as a "witch Hunt" and spoke late in the hearing. Hunter and site manager, Jim McBride, both testified, "...that no major health problems have been detected in dump employees"

Chamber of Commerce representative, Mike Rubic said, " The facility projects a bad image for Santa Maria Valley and lowers property values".

The Santa Maria Valley Developers submitted a letter stating, "We object to the state insistence that Santa Barbara County becoming the toxic dumping ground for Southern California." In a nut shell all who spoke at the hearing except for Hunter, McBride and the State Health Department representative, were against the dump. Unfortunately, the State Health Department ruled the day!

TIME MAGAZINE

The front cover page of Time Magazine on Oct. 14th read along with excellent graphic art, "THE POISONING OF AMERICA '85-TOXIC WASTES ". The author of the article did an exceptional job in describing the general situation and the small community of Casmalia and its surroundings, but he missed two major problems at Casmalia Resources. First, the accelerated evaporation systems consisting of farm sprinkler pipe on nine major areas at the site to dispose of waste into the air and surrounding valleys. Second, the use of the Zimpro Wet Air Oxidation machine which was being run without permits and was processing toxins it was never designed for and was also steaming these hot wastes up into the air. He printed the usual public relation scam from the full-time public relations employee, that I was getting tired of hearing, "We don't view us as the problem, but part of the solution." But the community did get good national attention. I managed to get another zinger in Time Magazine and thus the national media against the county about the earlier request in 1984 for an injunction and the county official telling me, "That I was not playing ball and had teed off all the county officials and that this is not the way we do it in Santa Barbara County." This was worth its weight in gold appearing in A the national media and adding pressure on county officials to act responsibly.

Years later at a high school class reunion I got some ribbing about me being willing to do anything, including trying to kill myself with toxic exposure, to get my photo into Time Magazine and the national media. Strangely enough Dr. Hart, the county health director, on Oct. 17th only three days after the Time Magazine publication, now knows where the odors are coming from and labels the dump a hazard and can't say it's safe." Another change of position by the county health director in response to public pressure. This actually did not improve his standing in my eyes or the communities, but only showed that he was wishy - washy and had no backbone.

PROTESTS AND RANKS SWELL

The Oct. 26 and 27th 1985 well-advertised protest at NTU and Back roads, set off a number of protests in the area against the dump site, and many other groups joined in. New groups included; Parents Against Casmalia Resources, Mother's for Peace, Citizens in League for Environmental Action Now, Greenpeace, Citizens for Public Health and Safety, Business Owners Against Toxic Pollution. Abalone Alliance, Toxic Tractorcaders, Casmalia Mothers Club, Health Professionals Against a Poison Environment. Students Against Casmalia Resources and Teachers Against Casmalia Resources.

Jerry Corlew, representing Casmalians Against Pollution and fresh from wining his court battle for his last arrest for blocking traffic, kicked off the event by marching the large assembled group up the road to the entrance gate to take up the dump sites' earlier offer of a tour of the site 15 people at a time. The security guard would not let them in and employees hid in the office trailer. While at the gate protesters tried to block a truck carrying toxics, but Sheriff's Deputies were on hand to let the truck through. Antonia Hernandez, a 75 years old resident of Casmalia for 45 years said she had been ill with headaches, sore throats, and ear aches since the dump opened. "Most of my friends are ill." Although she was not arrested, she said, she would be willing to go to jail as a symbol of her belief the dump is unsafe." The event continued for two days and according to news reports about 2,000 people attended.

Various other smaller vigil protests were held in Santa Maria at the city hall on Nov. 4, 85 and on April 4 and 11th 1986. These events helped to keep the subject in the news and were extremely important to the community effort. The community kept hammering and hammering!

CHAPTER 8

J. DAVID A PONZI CONNECTION AND BIRDS OF A FEATHER FLOCK TOGETHER

PONZI SCHEME AS A BLUE PRINT

Toxic waste was not the only irregular route to extreme riches. These other routes became entwined with the Casmalia Toxic Dump and its owner Kenneth Hunter, not only in terms of A methods, but with wedding bells. It is amazing how these other scams also fit the mold of the toxic waste business. High powered political and social contacts, lavish donations, twists and turns with regulators at all levels and attorneys making threats were all parts of the schemes. Casmalia Resources had the same make up as these historic scams to make as much money as fast as possible. The ball had to keep rolling for them to be successful. But for Hunter, the entanglement was a public relations blunder. It solidified the distaste for Hunter as a bottom feeder in the eyes of most Santa Barbara County residents. I was both shocked and elated when I heard the news of the upcoming wedding of Nancy Hover and Kenneth Hunter. It was excellent news for the community in its efforts against the dump site. I decided to make the most of the opportunity.

In Boston, prior to World War II, Charles Ponzi who had gone by the name of Bianchi in Canada and had spent time in Canadian prisons for forging signatures on checks, later made the name Ponzi infamous in the United States. Ponzi in the United States hit upon the idea of buying and selling International Postal Reply Coupons which varied in value based on the country's monetary exchange rates. But in his new scheme he did not even bother to purchase the coupons. He merely paid old customers with new customer money that came in. To be effective he had to keep the ball rolling. He had to attract affluent citizens to his scheme so he became a person who gave large amounts to charities and carried around large amounts of cash on his person as well as sporting around in a chauffeured limousine. He offered 50 percent return if they left their money in for 45 days and 100 percent for 90 days. In Boston he was at first considered a financial genius.

He kept no books, just notes promising to pay people a certain amount after a certain amount of time. Whenever questioned he use the excuse that he didn't want people to learn his secrets of trading. His key employee was his public relations man who kept the wolves away from the door. Like any true con man, he got his kicks out of keeping his cool and coming up with new lies at every turn. When he was on a roll, Ponzi acquire an interest in an established bank, bought an export-import company and dreamed of other acquisitions. But the ball for Ponzi did not keep rolling. His public relations man deserted him, government accountants swarmed over his IOUs. At first, they were thrown for a loop by the bookkeeping or lack of it. Long lines of angry creditors demanded the return of their money, but Ponzi remained calm, as he assured them, they would get their funds back. Auditors eventually found that he was three million short. Ponzi eventually went back to jail, still believing in his ability to pay everyone back.

J. DAVID COMPANY'S BEGINNINGS

Years went by in the United States, and although many small Ponzi schemes were tried, nothing quite so grand appeared, until about 1979 in San Diego, California. From the beginning many in the know in San Diego felt that Mr. Dominelli was running a Ponzi scheme. Nothing came together such as his visible track record on investments compared to his outstanding return on investments. Originally, Dominelli did his trading through Nancy Hoover, a sales associate for Bache in the San Diego area and the former Mayor of Del Mar, a small suburb of San Diego. The couple was later referred to by the San Diego media as Capitan Money and the Golden Girl. But Dominelli did very little trading in his high flying career. It was clearly a Ponzi scheme. Hoover, would later become his girlfriend and close confidant. Dominelli made good use of lawyers who made threats to some of those talking about their suspicions of a Ponzi scheme. People outside California became increasingly suspicious. Many individuals made J. David their investigation project. Many made inquires with various regulators telling them that Dominelli had top political and social contacts and paid investors 50 percent on their money. But for some reason regulators stayed away. Dominelli made various turns, twists, and maneuvers to avoid regulators. Talk of a Ponzi scheme and money laundering escalated, but Dominelli had an outstanding public relations person in the form of Nancy Hoover who had all the attributes that he was lacking. She ran with the liberals in the San Diego area and was extremely social. Jerry Dominelli was a conservative and quite the opposite in behavior. Together they seemed unbeatable. It was at this time they started a $50 million dollar spending spree while giving to charities. They both loved expensive autos and acquired many of them. The luxury items included ski condominiums, lavish estates, race and sports cars, racehorses, jewelry and furs. She was a good socializer and Dominelli was not. They gave away expensive cars to many them. So in many ways Jerry had a public relations manager who was more effective than in the original Ponzi scheme of Charles Ponzi. Lawyers and accountants kept the regulators away. The ball kept rolling with money coming in and good returns going out. It is estimated that well over $200 million was invested in the five-year period.

Strangely enough the J. David clash-with regulators was with Missouri regulators and not with those in California. They questioned whether the offerings were registered securities. Soon regulators in California took up the cause. This was when Dominelli decided to make a turn and trade in only interbank foreign currency trading. To accomplish this he set up a shell bank on the Caribbean island of Montserrat. It was perfect and fit his method of operations. It was unregulated and was just what he wanted.

The FBI started to investigate J. David as a Ponzi scheme in 1984, but closed the investigation a short time later after Dominelli assured everyone they were just looking for drug money. But it was reopened as J. David started to collapse. The enterprise had many supporters and friends in high places, so the FBI was hesitant to proceed with the investigation. Rodger Hedgecock, the new mayor of San Diego received most of his funding from J. David. Also, J. David had high powered national legal supporters. Between 1982 and 1984 Dominelli took in $200 million for the foreign currency program. 1983 was a wonderful year for J. David and associates.

It was also at this time that J. David opened its London Office. Investors would get a receipt and a thank you note from the London office. Dominelli sponsored the British-based Fitzpatrick auto racing team. But these showy efforts caused the Bank of England to consider an investigation of J. David. Mr. Yarry, an associate of Dominelli, decided to move operations to Lugano, Switzerland to avoid an audit. Dominelli and Hoover, at the home base in San Diego remained cool with many December parties and gifts, but things begin to unravel. They, however, were cool to the very end. Charles Ponzi would have been proud of their behavior.

J. DAVID DECLINE

At the end of December 1983 checks started to bounce. The bottom line was that the ball did not keep rolling. Sales people at J. David had to calm outraged investors who could not cash their checks. Rent had not been paid for the J. David office complex.

Health insurance premiums had not been paid. As a true con man, Dominelli used one excuse after another for the bouncing checks, but the run on the office became an avalanche. Lines of irate investors were outside the office, some waving guns. Lawyers threatened legal action. Employees were being terminated. People were now predicting an imminent collapse. Well into the new year J. David formally liquidated and a Bankruptcy Trustee was appointed. Against the judge's orders, Dominelli made a quick flight out of the country to the British West Indies Island of Monsterrat which housed his shell bank. While in Montserrat he made one last desperate effort to save himself and J. David with a call to New York's Joe Bonnano, leader of a reputed Mafia Family, in an effort to get a loan, but instead he ended up losing his last $125,000 for an upfront fee and no loan. When he was finally asked to leave, he made another flight to a close-by British island, but was shuffled back to Miami by authorities. He was handcuffed at the airport by authorities and returned to California. His bail was set at $5 million.

The crash also brought with it political consequences as the investigation shifted to the political arena with the focus on San Diego Mayor Rodger Hedgecock and the money from J. David tunneled into his campaigns. The California Fair Political Practices Commission filed a record $1.2 million suit against Hedgecock, Hoover and Dominelli. The Grand Jury in turn indicted Hedgecock, Hoover, Deominelli on 15 counts of perjury for their roles in Hedgecock's 1983 campaign. They had dumped $357,000 into his campaign. Legal actions continued for several years. Dominelli eventually pleaded guilty in 1985 to fraud and tax evasion in connection to the Ponzi scheme and was sentenced to 20 years in federal prison. Nancy was looking at a possible similar sentence. Her trial was pending! She was eventually given a 10 year sentence in federal prison. After her conviction Kenneth Hunter, her new husband, spent over $2 million to get her sentence reduced to just under three years.

As with all fairy-tales they must come to an end at some point and the Golden Girl had already set her sights on another prince charming multimillionaire from Montecito California by the name of Kenneth Hunter. Hunter, the toxic dump owner, had joined the likes of other Montecito residents in the plush suburb of Santa Barbara such as billionaire Harold Simmons, who had financed many Republican campaigns, Ty Warner, the creator of Beanie Babies in the 1990's, and race car legend Andy Granatelli. It would be the perfect neighborhood for Nancy if she could avoid jail time!

WEDDING BELLS

Santa Barbara News and Review said it best in their news story "Wedding Bells and Noxious Smells - Ken Hunter Faces the Music". Kenneth and Nancy filed a marriage certificate with the County of Santa Barbara on Oct. 3, 1985 and the ceremony was performed by retired Judge Frank Kearney at the Santa Barbara County Court House. An earlier event was rumored to have been cancelled on September 21st at the All Saints by the Sea Church because of fear of adverse publicity. It was smart that they did because the entire community of Casmalia would have attended and we would have turned it into another protest! To this day I question the wisdom of Hunter' decision to marry as it did wonders for the community's public relation efforts and was a blow to the dump's image.

FAMILY TRAIN TRIP TO SAN DIEGO

It was summer time and our family of four now needed a break. John, our son, was five and, our daughter, Meghan had just turned two. I certainly did need a break and my now constant off and on bouts with bronchial asthma had worn my health down. What better age for the kids to take a train trip? We could go and see the sights in San Diego such San Diego Wild Animal Zoo Park and Marine World. Of course, I had a more secret, obsessive and sinister visitor agenda-how about the

San Diego Court House? A little bird had told me about one of many upcoming Nancy Hoover Hunter hearings.

On a warm and sunny summer day, after parking our car in the depot parking lot, we all boarded the train in Santa Barbara for the trip down the coast to San Diego. It was a perfect day for an outing and I was carrying Meghan. She was all smiles and John was shooting ahead of us as the conductor helped us all onto the train car. The kids loved the new experience. This was their first train ride. We were soon speeding along watching the coastal ocean views sweep by the train windows. It was a memorable family togetherness day. After picking up our rental car at the San Diego Old Town Depot we spent the afternoon touring the harbor area and made arrangements for our room at the Embassy Suites. It was a great trip for our children and the A San Diego Zoo was outstanding. The following day was spent at Marine World. But our last day, the most important to me, was a short visit to the Court Complex.

At the complex my first plan was to rattle the newlywed's cage and it worked beautifully. I was carrying my two year old daughter as they were walking toward and passed me. The shock on their faces to see me in far off San Diego was worth a million dollars. My second purpose was to engage one of the TV stations that were set up in the Court Complex Plaza. It was perfect for a one on one interview about Nancy Hoover Hunter and her new husband as well as about his toxic waste dump site. By this time I must say I had become an expert at one on one TV interviews, so I laid it on thick and that gave me great satisfaction!

TOXIC WASTE DISPOSAL JUST ANOTHER SCAM

On our train ride north back to Santa Barbara the kids had fallen asleep as we again traveled along the beautiful Pacific Ocean, but as usual I was obsessing and contemplating. Looking out the train window I noted a flock of sea birds busying themselves diving for a school of fish. The old adage "Birds of a feather flock together" is true at so many levels. Kenneth Hunter and

Nancy Hover Hunter were meant for each other. They both were and had been engaging in a lot of scams that would have made Charles Ponzi proud. Casmalia Resources and the toxic waste facility had all the attributes of a first-class scam. First, it had a public relations director that kept both the environmental falsehoods intact and the money rolling into its coffers. The organization used high-powered lawyers to make behind-the-scenes threats to keep any public criticism quiet. The operation had played the different levels of oversight and regulation like a A new fiddle to the point of no regulation at all. Some of the assertions such as "no water under the site" and "we cannot tell were the odors originate" were beyond the belief of ordinary intelligence. They exercised political influence from some lowly local supervisors up to and including the state governor. They were attempting to make as much money as fast as possible. All of these were attribute of a first class scam. Much still lay ahead for me and the community I thought as I fell asleep watching the Pacific crashing onto the coast line.

CHAPTER 9

GOING VISUAL AND THE TIDE STARTS TO SLOWLY TURN

Perhaps those poor folks in Casmalia have something? As the fumes flowed into neighboring Orcutt from the coastal foothills and the angry calls flooded the Air Pollution Control District office I started to get requests from Local civic groups for presentations and it was at this time I made the decision to have a video prepared to take with me to these presentations. I had just completed a lengthy commentary for the central coast newspapers including one in Dewayne Holmdahal's and the Casmalia School's Supervisorial district which would make a great narrative for the video. This I adjusted to fit the needs of a video and then found a local company that prepared TV commercials. Next, I needed an official sounding voice and was fortunate to readily find a Disk Jockey from a local radio station who was favorable to our cause, and who agreed to be our voice for the video. It proved to be quite helpful in our efforts. I tool it with me to many social and civic groups and could tell from the public response that the public was now more favorable to our cause. This was especially true when they perceived it impacting them directly!

A GRANDIOSE SOLUTION

I closed both my video presentations and my commentaries with the same grandiose solution and message: "Casmalia's story is a tragic and graphic example of the failure to effectively shift regulatory control to the local levels. I feel strongly that national problems deserve national recognition and national solutions. It is time for a national effort and a commitment, as great as our commitment to space exploration, to create a strong federal presence including quasi-governmental agencies actually running modern, well equipped disposal facilities away from populated areas. Universities should be encouraged to create Departments of Waste Disposal just as they were encouraged to expand their Science and Engineering departments in the early '60s. Let us make Casmalia truly the last one--the last A private unregulated toxic landfill."

(But with just me hoping our grand dream would someday move forward and come true) Our attorneys. In May of 1985, Richard Brenneman and Cory Birnberg from San Francisco, working in our behalf, filed suits for over $1 billion in damages against the dump and its principal owner Kenneth Hunter contending, "air and water outside the dump's boundaries have been tested and found to contain hazardous materials at unacceptable levels and that these materials will continue to migrate off site to the detriment of the environment and human health which creates a risk of substantial harm to those who have been and are being exposed.7'All these events; law suits, hearings, presentations, news reports, Grand Jury efforts, and protests added to pressure on regulators at all levels.

COUNTY DEMAND

This pressure manifested itself in the county government, when all of a sudden, the county supervisors and the District Attorney for the county, could unanimously agree that the noxious odors needed to stop. My god, the county DA now said, after half the county was in an uproar, that he would pursue a court action under "public nuisance" provisions to require the dump to stop taking any materials that produce odors.

Now let's see- he does not take action when students and staff are chased out of a public school building when no oxygen is available to breath, but he does after enough people start to complain. The state of California Department of Health Care Services still refused to take any action unless there was a "proven health hazard". The action and the order from the local supervisors came just in time for the special A hearing in Orcutt by the Senate Toxics Committee. Larry Appel from the North County Resource Management Department now also tells the board that the site has gone well beyond its 1976 permit and it should cut back its operations or apply for a new permit. This report is left for debate at the next supervisor's meeting.

The demand letter also noted that, "...the recent oil spraying and aeration treatment has not solved the odor problem nor does it believe that a treatment system will operate without aggravating the odor problem." The State Health Services Director, Dr. Ken Kizer, told supervisors he would make a decision about a 501 hearing on Friday, but Friday came and went with no decision from the state. Enforcing the order and demand with legal action becomes the next issue for the county. Kenneth Hunter responds to the order and demand stating it is "arbitrary and capricious" and leaves his 4,000 Southern California customers with nowhere to go to dispose of their waste. He thus refused to curtail operations. By the day of the hearing the supervisors had received well over 700 angry letters about the dump site. With this response from Hunter and the angry letters, the board of supervisors voted on Oct. 15, 1985 to initiate a court action which it had threatened the prior Monday.

The report given to the supervisors from the Resource Management Department pointed out that the site had grown from its 1976 assessment by 62 percent of liquid waste and 2,000 percent in solid waste. The disposal area had grown without permits from 168 acres to 252 acres. The number of trucks per day had increased from 60 to 130.

On Oct. 21, 1985 the county also files a writ of mandate against the State Department of Health Services because of its refusal to close the

Casmalia Resources Toxic dumpsite. The writ has the effect of making the state prove that the site is not a health hazard.

On Jan. 16, 1986 the County Planning Commission unanimously decides to pull the dump's permit to operate and gives them 10 days to appeal to the Board of Supervisors. The decision was based on the report that the dump had violated its 1976 conditional use permit by operation on land for which no permit had been obtained and by having too many trucks traveling to the facility each day. Commission chairwoman, Nancy Johnson, gave attorney Cooney, representing Casmalia Resources hell. That made my day. He was the same attorney who had sent me the threatening letter.

GRAND JURY HITS STATE HEALTH DEPARTMENT HARD

On the prior Dec. 11 the state health department had conducted a kangaroo hearing in Santa Maria that gave the go-ahead allowing a new toxic waste neutralization system to deal with all the new waste. The county, however, refused to approve the cement pad for the new unit. On Jan 26, 1986 the Grand Jury sent their colorful prostitution letter. They started by telling the state director, Dr. Kizer, that the hearing process "had been prostituted". It was apparent that the state officials had already approved the system before the hearing was held. It is the Grand Jury's opinion, "...the DOH'S presentation of the so-called statement of facts and operations document was little more than a sales presentation on behalf of Casmalia Resources". They further stated the presentation, "... could not have been more biased in favor of the Casmalia.

Resources facility than if the presentation had been presented by the Casmalia Resources staff itself". The letter was certainly right on the mark. Time it was well known that the state had a vested interest in finding a spot for waste from Southern California which had much more political clout than rural Santa Barbara County.

On June 8, 1986, just in time for the "501 Closure hearing set for June 12 and 13 at Lakeview School in Orcutt, the Grand Jury restated its preliminary report from the prior fall with more detail. They again called for the site's closure stating, "…it's a real and present, immediate and substantial endangerment to public health." They pointed out a 1983 EPA report that found groundwater and not just surface water had contaminates exceeding federal drinking water standards of substances ranging from chloride to lead. They also pointed out that there were geologic fractures under the northern third of the site that would allow flow toward the Santa Maria Valley.

HEALTH STUDY RELEASED IN LOS ANGELES TIMES

Also, on June 8th one of our attorneys, Robert Sulnick released, on behalf of the community, a summary of the results of the Casmalia Health Study of 167 residents, and a control group of 49 residents from Arroyo Grande. In the small town of Casmalia they found abnormally high occurrences of respiratory and central nervous system problems and elevated white blood cell counts. Researchers said, "…the tests showed the presence of toxins in residents' blood and urine and evidence of attempts by their immune systems to cope with the chemical assault."

The study was conducted by toxicologist Jan Schienle of California State University, Northridge and four physicians and the difference between the two groups was "statistically significant". Among the findings with comparisons:

1. Sixty percent of Casmalians, as opposed 2% of the control group, showed chronic respiratory problems.
2. Neurological symptoms were 15 times higher than the control group.
3. 85 percent of Casmalia residents showed abnormal pulmonary function ranging from a loss of 30% to 90% of lung capacity.
4. 85 percent had respiratory tract irritations, such as shortness of breath and coughing.

5. Two -thirds had elevated liver enzymes indicating that the livers were trying to detoxify the blood.

Prior to the upcoming 501 hearing, the State Health Department subpoenaed the toxicologist and doctors who worked on the tests, in an effort to get the data. It is privileged information to be used in an upcoming suit against the dump site and, Robert Sulnick, our attorney, vowed to fight the subpoenas. Fortunately, they served the subpoenas at the wrong address which gave our community more time. Almost a year later on Jan. 9, 1987 Los Angeles Superior Court Judge Richard Torress ruled that Sulnick would not have to turn over his clients' medical data to the state Department of Health Services. The judge ruled along with Sulnick's arguments that if the state wanted the results so badly, it should have funded its own study. It was confidential information to be used in his clients' pending law suit. Sulnick said his clients did not think they had much to gain by releasing the study to either state or county officials. He added they, "…don't have much faith in the state or county". To say the least, this argument was an understatement as the community had understandably developed a real and lasting hatred of all county and state personnel.

The county's share of dump tax revenue now stood at $2.5 million per year which proved to < make it much harder for the county to stand firm. Legal issues now develop with the authority of the of the county to regulate toxic dumps. These roadblock issues would later have to be resolved at the State Supreme Court level.

CHAPTER 10

LARGE CASMALIA SCHOOL RALLY AND LATER RESPONSE TO HUNTER'S DUMP TOUR

LARGE STATE WIDE RALLY IN SCHOOL YARD

Citizens Alliance for a Safe Environment (CASE) lead by my good friend Kathy Hoxie went into high gear to prepare for one of the largest events yet, set for May 4, 1986 in opposition to our unwanted neighbor. It was to be billed as the "People's Rally Against Toxic Waste" and was to be held on a Saturday on the school grounds. Other supporters and sponsors included the Environmental Defense Fund, the Sierra Club, the United Farm Workers, and Concerned Neighbors in Action of Riverside. Los Angeles Mayor Tom Bradley was set to speak at 10:00 AM who was sure to take on Gov. George Deukmejian, his opponent for governor, for his record or lack of one on toxic waste. Hoxie said the governor had been invited but aides have indicated several times that he would not attend. Other speakers would include Sen. Gary Hart, Assembly members Jack O'Connell and Eric Seastrand as well as Lt. Governor Leo T. McCarthy. She also said, "… the rally will be a prelude to the state-sponsored 501 hearing to be held June 12-13 at Lakeview School in Orcutt." She was unable to estimate the number of people who might attend but said, "… groups from Kern County, Silicon Valley, the Landcaster-Palmdale area, Sacramento, San Diego and the McColl dump site in Orange County have indicated they would attend Saturday's activities." The main purpose of the event she said, "…is to increase Santa Barbara County's awareness that Casmalia Resources is still going strong." The event, she added, "…will unite groups throughout the county and the state in our fight against toxics. This dump isn't closed, it's operating and there really hasn't been any kind of cutback at all out there."

Tom Bradley started his presentation with an old and appropriate chant "We are madder than hell and we aren't going to take it any longer". It was an excellent rallying call and it helped to focus the local community for that long battle that sill lay ahead and our eventual trip to Sacramento. Bradley was dressed in a white jogging suit and I met him briefly for a hand shake and a thank you to him as he went through the school building out to the stage. The mayor had challenged Governor Deukmejain in that year's gubernatorial race and boy did he hit him hard on his handling of toxic waste issues. He commended opponents of Casmalia Resources and said, "… it was only through their perseverance that any action was taken in reference to the scheduled 501 hearing. We had forced this on the state Department of Health Services." But Bradley went on to caution dump opponents, "You and I know that the battle is not over. Casmalia dump has become a symbol for this whole state, indeed, I think for the nation. It represents both the worst and as well as the best. The worst is represented by callous disregard shown by state and other government officials responsible for our health and dump site regulations. On the other hand, anh-dump people have represented the best by their perseverance and determination for asking for protection, demanding hearings and holding rallies." Bradley also mentioned that Deukmejian had, "…vetoed 21 toxic-waste bills while receiving $500,000 in campaign contributions from the toxic waste industry".

Lt. Gov. Leo McCarthy in his presentation stated, "…as the foot soldiers in the war against toxic poisoning in the state I commend you all". Other speakers such a John O'Connor of the National Campaign Against Toxic Hazards from Connecticut stated, "toxics are the nation's number one hidden health problem and there are at least 50 deaths per day in the nation related to toxic problems and yet there was little national concern. Imagine if terrorist killed 50 people per day. What would the national response be?" Along with other speakers from around the state, Senator Gary Hart, Assemblyman Jack O'Connell, local Fifth Dist. Supervisor Toru Miyoshi gave us rousing and supportive presentations, but Supervisor DeWayne Homldhal, our usual nemesis, was absent as usual. He was smart to be absent as I am sure he would have received rousing boos! Perhaps he was smarter than he looked?

The school rally was a smashing success and most importantly got us state-wide coverage on national and state media outlets. But Hunter would not be outdone and by May 8th he had his public relations department give a presentation for the news media with his own video and bus tour to the front of the Wet Air Oxidation unit, as well as having the production professionally prepared by his paid public relations employees.

HUNTER PRESS TOUR AND RESPONSE TO RALLY

He started his own personnel appearance at this event by saying, "… I have a great deal of sympathy for residents of the town of Casmalia, but I still plan to testify at the upcoming 501 hearing". Hunter, also said, "…I am confident the dump will remain open after the hearing." He didn't know at the time that because of communications I had received I was just as dismayed that he was right; the dump would remain open after the hearing. After his brief comments other employees of the toxic waste facility led about 20 Central Coast and Southern California reporters on a three hour bus tour of the site. He was available when they all returned for the video and show narrative. The tour appeared to have two purposes, both related to positive media coverage. The first to get their side of the story about the upcoming hearing and second to puff up the Wet Air Oxidation system that had in fact no scientific basis and only shot toxic steam up into the air to get rid of toxic waste.

But before he got into the other main purpose he again said, "...I do not think the dump is responsible for making people sick and I can cite my own employee health histories". This, investigators for the community found, was false. He also responded to a reporter saying, "The Casmia School closure was monetarily inspired. Those who have filed a lawsuit against the facility are merely seeking the millions of dollars that may be obtained if such a suit is successful."

Then, standing in front of the building housing the facilities Zimpro Wet Air Oxidation Unit, he Proclaimed, "Zimpro is the most futuristic way of processing Hazardous waste in the state. The company wants to install a second Zimpro Unit with hearings tentatively planned after the 501 hearing next month." General manager Jim McBride said, "... the dump s in business to protect the environment. Casmalia was selected because of 1,500 and 3,000 feet of shale layers under the site. The dump site owns about 5,000 acres and operates on about 170." Many of these figures were false and he forgot to tell that they expanded dump site acreage because of other neighboring ranch owners not wanting land next to the dump site. The 170 acres that it operated on was closer to 240 acres with no permits.

McBride then gave his explanation and showcase of the wonderful Zimpro high pressure system that he contended, "...converts toxic molecules into smaller and less toxic ones." He forgot to explain that it was merely toxic steam they were blowing up into the air into neighboring canyons and valleys. He also gave a false list of materials on-site such as oil and gas, aircraft plating materials, but carefully left out cyanide and pesticides.

CASMALIA SUITS WERE A RESPONSE TO HARM

I could hardly wait to respond to this hogwash on the day of May 11th which was planned for a response. Using my one on one process, I worked with each station and newspaper separately that arrived in response to our calls to cover the story. We now had substantial pull with the media and the turnout was great.

I started my comments by saying, " I am responding to the slanderous remarks made by the heartless owner, Mr. Hunter of the toxic dump site, on his tour of his facility. Lawsuits against Casmalia Resources were filled in an effort to regain lost property values caused by the proximity to the toxic waste facility and to reimburse nearby residents for the harm and exposure. This lawsuit has been brought by approximately 200 residents and the school district. Last week Hunter had the audacity to say during a tour for reporters, "those involved in the suit are merely seeking the millions of dollars they may get if successful." My response was. "I strongly object, on behalf of the community, to these unwelcome and unjustified comments."

The media reported, "…The school principal, who is a law school graduate, also said that the two suits filed in Santa Maria Superior Court have been combined. Lead attorney for the suit, which has not yet been heard, is Robert Sulnick, a law school professor at Loyola University in Los Angeles. Residents in the town of Casmalia are stranded because they cannot sell their property because of the town's closeness to the dump and others who rent, often live in poverty. Their property is worth zero".

I can give you examples, "One day I met the county inspector in front of the school when the odors and fumes were atrocious and he said to me, with a straight face, that he could not smell a thing. He then went around town telling everyone that it was a psychological thing. A county nurse at one point called Jerry Corlew, a resident, and told him he needed to seek counseling. He listens to his baby struggling to breathe at night and he gets angry, real angry, and he is not alone. Jerry was later arrested at the entrance of the dump for blocking traffic. Jerry would move, but he rents and only pays dirt cheap rent for California's expensive Central Coast area at $300 per month. Similar property would be $1,200 anywhere else. He runs a fishing tackle business out of his garage."

I went on to say, "At one point the main street in town was covered with FOR SALE signs, but they eventually all came down because no one in their right mind would want to live in Casmalia under these conditions. They are all trapped. Many people hope that the company will eventually buy out the town and relocate the citizens."

I also emphatically said, "...the lawsuit was filed because of higher-than-normal rates of health problems for the estimated 200 people of Casmalia. Just in a five-year period there have been six lung-related deaths, four from cancer, one from leukemia and several stillbirths and children born with birth defects."

Concerning the upcoming 501 hearing to be held on June 12-13, "...we need a strong turnout because the person holding the hearing and who will make the ultimate decision, Dr. Kizer, and the State of California have a vested interest in keeping this site open. They have few options for taking the cleaned up waste from other toxic dumps elsewhere in the state. It will be an up hill fight!"

I continued, " I strongly object and oppose Dr.Kizer's decision to require speakers to submit summaries in advance of the hearing. If you are holding a hearing, you don't limit the information. This is a public issue and state officials should be able to take the heat. They shouldn't be allowed to weed out the people they don't want to hear from."

I closed by saying, "Odors still affect the school as they did last summer and fall. When warm weather arrives Santa Maria and Oructt will again experience odors and fumes from the dump. Living out here close, there has been no change."

CASMALIA WATER DISTRICT TO LOSE INSURANCE

For the small community of Casmalia another negative issue and problem develops, which may put additional pressure on County Supervisors and point out the seriousness of the situation for the entire county. This problem was shared with county supervisors at their May 20, 1986 meeting by Mr. Kenneth Vaniter, the CCSD manager. The Casmalia Community Service District received notice that "Casmalia class I dump's Toxics and water don't mix" and that premiums would increase from $1,000 per year to $6,023 per year.

Interestingly enough the Casmalia Communities' water well was located five miles away in the Santa Maria Valley and the well water was pumped up to the community in the coastal foothills. The import here was that they were talking about a Santa Maria/ Orcutt water wells and not one in the Casmalia watershed. Transcontinetal Insurance spokesman William Mallone, insisted that, "… where Cass I dumps like Casmalia are concerned, depending on the geology of the area, 50 miles away may be too close. Problems related to Class I dump sites are serious, and make insurance companies exceedingly susceptible to bodily injury or property damage claims." I am sure all the issues with other dumps around the state, such as the McColl site, where the water in the entire valley was not useable was, in fact, the reason for the increase in premiums.

In a letter, prior to an upcoming supervisors meeting, to "good old boy" Supervisor DeWayne Holmdahl, the dump site advocate, from Mr. Vaniter he pointed out, "…that some kind of help from the county was essential because the local district of 65 customers could not bear this increase. Perhaps the District could be helped out financially or added to the county insurance? Without help this issue could force the CCSD to dissolve and leave the county holding the bag." Supervisor Bill Wallace asked at the meeting, "What would keep the county's own insurance company from cancelling as we are not such good clients either?" It was unanimously decided to postpone the matter until June 9th, the first meeting after the upcoming elections, to give the county time to study the problem in more detail.

CHAPTER 11

"501" STATE CLOSURE HEARING WITH A BOMB THREAT

EVENTS LEADING UP TO THE HEARING

The public in Casmalia, Orcutt, and Santa Maria, as well as me, were eagerly awaiting the 501 closure hearing. Initially, I had high hopes of success until I received a communication from an attorney. Unfortunately, I was made privy to communications between the State Health Director, Dr. Kenneth Kizer, and Environmental Defense Fund attorney David Roe from Berkley, California. The letters were shocking to say the least. I was surprised the Health Director would I put this into a letter to anyone. In essence it said," I have NO INTENTION to consider a facility shutdown at Casmalia; the purpose of the Casmalia 501 hearing IS NOT to establish whether facts warrant closing the Casmalia facility. The Department DOES NOT intend to hold a judicial type of hearing at this time. CERTAIN INSPECTION REPORTS which relate to current enforcement actions WILL NOT be available to the public. With these limitations, the public was being misled by the main person to be running the upcoming hearing. Politically, from the governor on down to the health director, they knew there was no other place to put toxic waste from Southern California and this was merely a gambit for additional time to move waste from the Los Angeles area to Casmalia. Reflecting on the J. David scam, it also made me wonder about money exchanging hands for political favors. After being made privy to this information, preparing for the upcoming hearings became a mental drag on my once high hopes of success. At this juncture I would have preferred not to have attended, but still a large attendance was important.

I did not share my reluctance with others, but my personal enthusiasm was severely curtailed by the statement in the letter from Kizer. He was the one person who would make the final decision and his decision was in before any facts were presented. No wonder Hunter was so confident on his dump tour that he would still be in business after the hearing and was planning the expansion of the Wet Air Oxidation Unit. This, further down the road, made it easy for me to both lead a protest against Kizer in nearby San Luis Obispo and to later attend one in far off Sacramento against he and the governor. Dr. Kizer and the governor were apparently so surrounded by political appointees that were "yes men" that he thought nothing of sending this incriminating letter. They were both nothing more than political cronies running a scam for campaign obligations and payments. The information dampened my spirits, but also pointed out the need for a super-large turnout of citizens, to make a media and political point! Turnout, turnout was our goal!

WORKSHOP IN PREPARATION FOR SPEAKERS

Normally my bronchial asthma would come and go and I would muff through it and continue to go to work each day, but I was having a severe bronchial asthma episode that did not seem to get better and I had to miss work for a few days, which was unusual for me. I always figured that if the school children could make it, I could certainly drag myself out to work. But on this Tuesday, May 20, 1986 I was unable to make it to the "flush out" workshop. It was to prepare everyone for the upcoming 501 hearing. It was just as well as my spirts were low with the illness and the letter from David Roe.

The workshop was conducted by Supervisor Toru Miyoshi and was a warm-up on how to testify at the hearing. All the panelists urged strong attendance, but all agreed that the deck was stacked against opponents of the toxic waste site. Attorney Dick Brenneman who represented

the school district and the community suggested that, "…all should complain about the format of the hearing itself such as lack of notice, the requirement that speakers submit a written summary in advance, as well as only 10 minutes to speak. How can you be limited to 10 minutes when you have eight years to talk about?" Mike Picker and Jodi Sparks from the Sacramento-based Toxic Assessment Group, both pointed out that the guidelines were outrageous to try and to cover both personal health issues plus lack of adequate air and water monitoring, and that much of the monitoring data was not shared with the public as it was supposedly held back for enforcement action that never seemed to occur. Picket also pointed out that the 501 hearing was established in 1980 as a method to keep the city of West Covina from closing the BKK toxic facility.

Attorney Richard Brenneman said that, "…there is still another legal step that can take place if we fail… a writ of mandate asking the appellate court to review the hearing could result in subpoenaing of the records previously not available. It's a long process, but ultimately we may be able to flush them out." It was an excellent plan for a back-up position. It was apparent to me that this hearing did not have a "snowball's chance in hell" of closing this toxic dump!

SUPERVISORS HAMMER OUT POSITION FOR 501

On May 19, 1986 at a regular board meeting, Chairman of the Board Toru Miyoshi tried to get supervisors to take a position-either for or against the dump site-but they declined. He followed the setback, however, with a letter to all the supervisors stating that, "people are suffering adverse health effects and loss of property value because of the Casmalia Toxic Dump." On the following Monday he still encountered opposition.

Santa Maria Chamber of Commerce spokesman Tim Mahoney cautioned board members that, it's was too early for the board to take a position because all the facts weren't. He felt a premature decision might bias the 501 hearing. Miyoshi, clearly at the end of his patience, countered to Mahoney by asking, "You mean they have to go into the hospital and fall over dead?" Not taking a position, he charged, would mean a total breakdown in credibility of the board to protect the people it serves. So, despite warnings from some present that they should wait, the board took a stand against the dump in preparation for the upcoming "501" hearing. In the meantime, they all agreed to send a letter to Dr. Ken kizer, explaining that "the burden of proving the facility is safe will be on the state's shoulders during the hearing. Since the board's authority to close down the site is limited, we expect the state to prove the site's safety." Miyoshi, as chairman, would read the board's letter at the hearing. At least the board had swayed with public opinion and was now somewhat working to help Casmalia. Dr. Lawrence Hart also spoke up at the supervisor's meeting and told the board members it has been,"…one of the most frustrating experiences of my professional career to get a Casmalia 501 hearing." As usual Dr. Hart could bend in the wind and his statement was the most disingenuous and false statement I had ever heard. He and his local health department were the main obstacles to protecting the health of local residences.

Apparently, Supervisor Bill Wallace from South County was reading the news reports concerning Casmalia because his comments echoed my statements and those of attorney Brennamen about objecting to speakers having to submit a written copy of their testimony weeks in advance. He said, "it isn't much of a live hearing…sounds like a closed hearing to me."

The Santa Barbara County Grand Jury also put in their views by suggesting, "The state and Dr.Kizer should provide an impartial panel to hear testimony at the hearing and not those connected with the state health department. Without safeguards, the outcome of the hearing might be vulnerable to outside influence and pressure from Toxic Waste Management special interests."

State Senator Gary Hart sent a letter to Miyoshi which said, "despite requests from your board, the county health office, myself and other legislators, Dr. Kenneth Kizer has for the past five months refused to hold a 501 hearing on the problems at Casmalia. It is a sad commentary on the Deukmejian administration that they are willing to respond to local concerns only when extremely pressured to do so. Second guess the outcome. I will err on the side of protecting health if there was some doubt about the health consequences of the dump." Quite a difference from his private communication in my file!

"501" IN NATIONAL SPOTLIGHT

The national media was focused on the first ever 501 hearing as it was gaveled to order, unfortunately and unknown to them, not clearing the way for the possible closure of the site as under state law only Dr. Kizer could make that decision and it was apparent from his early written comments that this was not going to happen. In effect it was a "staged dog and pony show" that he was forced to put on because of public pressure.

The poor abused Dr. Hart, the County Health Director, who was one of the first of many to speak, stuck with the new county line from his bosses, the supervisors, that he thought, it was the responsibility of the state to prove that the site did not present health problems, rather than residents proving that it did. This was all well and good, but he then continued on whining that he had been precluded from doing his duty as a public health officer because attorneys for Casmalians suing the dump had not released pertinent health-survey information. He skimmed over the fact that his own health surveyors had alienated the local population so much that they would have nothing to do with Dr. Hart or his department. He also omitted the fact that the summary of the health survey had been run in every local paper, plus the Los Angeles Times, or that he had made an effort to get the toxicologist in charge of the survey fired from her professorship, just a few minor omissions in his presentation to say the least!

The schedule of speakers for Thursday night included Senator Gary Hart and Drs. Steve Williams, Dan Du Coffe, Zane Gard and Dr. Collatz. Those representing now more than 60 Santa Maria area doctors would speak on Friday morning against the continued operation of the dump. Only the one doctor paid for by the dump owner testified in favor of its safety.

FRIDAY'S BOMB THREAT DELAYS "501"

The hearing got off to a slow start on Friday because a man, described with a middle-aged voice, called in a bomb threat to 911 just as the hearing was to start. The packed room was vacated and folks sent outside and then it was carefully searched. The police said, "it was false and unfounded, but a serious offense." After the search, the room it was refilled and the show started again. When asked, Dr. Hart said, "Yes stress can be a factor that causes threats such as the one we just experienced."

My personal opinion that I did not state or share with others was that I was surprised that some serious injury had not already occurred with poor people trapped next to a large toxic dump. I also later wondered if Dr. Hart's positions and actions at a later Board of Supervisors' meeting, although couched in supposed concern for the poor folks' plight in Casmalia, was really motivated by a concern for his own personal safety after the bomb threat? Many of the similar health problems, including respiratory ailments. These problems were greatly alleviated after Williams advised them to move to Santa Maria." He also added, "…the man had a metallic chemical odor on his clothing." Dr. Ted Callahan, an obstetrician in Santa Maria for a decade, said, "…in recent years the miscarriage rate goes up and up and up." Dr. John Berry testified, "…there were three cases of leukemia in local children last year. Ordinarily, one such case is reported about every other year. I believe the dump is partly responsible for the increase. "

I stated when my turn rolled around, "those health problems have not gone away since the 1984 closure of our school. I go to work sick.

The kids come to school sick. We continue on." The dump had hired experts to testify and brought in all their employees who stuck with the false line that they were all in excellent health. It was at this time that I recognized the dump employee, as he testified, who had tried to kill me by running me off the road.

In a comment typical of many Orcutt folks Debra Vaudrin spoke and stated, "We feel the panel is having us prove to them the site is unsafe, but we should be asking them to prove that it is safe". Her feelings were graphically illustrated at a noontime rally. Citizens paraded effigies of Kizer, Kenneth Hunter and 4th District Supervisor DeWayne Holmdahl, who in the past was criticized for not working hard enough against Casmalia Resources and for making statements in support of the dump site. A fifth district Supervisor, a long-time dump opponent, read a letter from the board saying, "…the burden of proof should fall on the state to prove the dump presents no health problems, rather than citizens proving that it is unsafe."

After the question to Dr. Hart at the hearing about stress and the bomb threat, Dr. Hart, at the next Board of Supervisor's meeting, brought up the idea of relocating Casmalia residents with state and federal money because the community was in a panic and the bomb threat was a symptom of the panic. The board supported this request and asked for an expeditious decision on the fate of the dump site. Unfortunately, the expeditious part of the request was long in coming. The bomb threat did have the effect of making Dr. Hart finally believe that this was a serious problem he was dealing with and it was not going away without upfront and honest action on his part.

It was at this time a brilliant group of investors wanted to re-open a long abandoned diatomaceous earth plant next to Casmalia. This required burning and plenty of ash being spewed into the air. This was the last straw for my loyal teacher's aide Paulette Postiff who had been rather politically quiet during the past few years. In her letter to the editor, she summed it up well, "We have been yelling for help for over two years and what do we get? More trouble with another plant to make the air worse. If anyone wonders why I don't move it's because we can't sell our house. It was up for sale for six months and we didn't get one phone call on it. No one will loan money to buy in Casmalia. Please don't listen to our county officials. Fight for clean air and water." The community's patience were now at the breaking point!

CHAPTER 12

THE GAVIOTA CONNECTION AND WESTERN MIGRATION

CASMALIA'S TENACITY SETS THE STAGE FOR WINNING THE BATTLE

All folks who traversed the American continent had to develop tenacity and the ability to succeed. Casmalia's population was no different and this was hard lined into their DNA.

I could see it every day in the children who went to our school in Casmalia. My own family had a tumultuous past that was a blue print for the American experience and Casmalia's experience. My, on again, off again, illnesses pattern was giving me wavering thoughts as my health went up and down about the correct direction to take with Gaviota's alluring connection. Tenacity helped me eventually make the right decision!

BEAUTIFUL AND PERFECT GAVIOTA SCHOOL

As you head north from Santa Maria toward Santa Barbara on the 101 Freeway the roadway passes through Gaviota Pass which is famous in early California history as the narrow pass in which the Spanish and Indians from Santa Barbara waited on high cliffs to ambush the Americans who were headed South to capture the city of Santa Barbara. Unfortunately for the Spanish and Indians laying in wait, the Americans took another route and came into Santa Barbara from the back dragging equipment down from the San Marcos Pass, a higher pass in the coastal range directly behind Santa Barbara.

Today, as you swing out along the roadway to the Pacific from the pass you behold the magnificent vista of the Pacific Ocean as you emerge. The original small Gaviota School site sits to the left of the highway. Now, immediately next the old site, sits a large oil refinery that services oil produced off the coast. When this oil production facility was built, the oil company paid to relocate the school, with no costs spared, to a new location in an oak tree studded valley in the coastal foothills far away from the production facility.

When the new school was completed, being a neighboring Principal/Superintendent from a similar sized school that also could service up to 60 students, I was invited along with others for a tour and open house. It was a school site to behold for me with its new parking facilities and fresh new Spanish style design. It was readily apparent that cost was no object when this was planned and built. It had classrooms, and also classrooms just for science, coupled with offices and various multipurpose rooms. It had everything you could want or need as an educator. These visions from my visit lingered in my mind and made me envious and made our relatively new Title I school, built to service poor students, look poorly in comparison. But, life was what it was and the years drifted by after this visit and in California, school funding being not fair, was also what it was and the Gaviota District was fortunate.

MY RESPITORY ILLNESS WORSENS

It was another typical day with mild odors around the school grounds and, as usual, I was working with a slight case of respiratory problems when the delivery truck arrived from the county school's office with a delivery of school mail. Glancing through the pile of communications I noted a form letter to me from the County Personnel Office. I pulled it apart and glanced at the content. It was an application and announcement that Gaviota School District was seeking a new Principal/Superintendent. Not considering it seriously, however, I did put it into my sport coat pocket to show to my wife, Pernelle, at home that night. Later that night I completely forgot about the flyer.

A few days later, my on and off again bronchial asthma became much worse and I decided to stay home from work and try to recover as well as go to the doctor. It was on this day at home I finally remembered the flyer in my pocket and decided to submit my application and resume.

The County Schools Personnel Office was handling all the screening of applicants. It was a day in which my spirits were down and it did not dawn on me that this had the potential to be a public relations blunder. It had not occurred to me, that after all the publicity, people in the media were watching for any news story and me in particular, dealing with this issue. My respiratory problems eventually subsided somewhat and back to my normal and usual routine I went.

But, within a few weeks, my respiratory problem was back and on top of it all I seemed to be running a temperature which was not the usual routine for my bouts of asthma. Luckily it began on a weekend, and started on a Friday and by Saturday I woke up in bed with an extremely high temperature. Unable to sleep that morning and destined for a day in bed, my mind began to wonder. It naturally wondered to my most favorite subject and also to whether I had made the correct decision to apply for the dream teaching and administrative position at Gaviota School District?

Having majored in history and having loved the subject from childhood, I knew my family history and ancestry in great detail. I also had spent many a long summer's days dragging my wife from one homestead to another across the United States following the path of my family's early migration to the Pacific from far off Scotland. There story I found was a microcosm of the American experience.

FROM THE CELTIC MIST AND THE HIGHLANDS

Our family history starts from out of the darkness of ancient history. Through the Celtic mist in 810 AD, stepped the son of chieftain Alpin who was leading the Scots in their struggle against the Picts and invading Vikings in the highlands of Scotland. Although Kenneth's father Alpin was a Scot he had a Pictish mother and the spelling of his Pictish name at the time was "Cinaeth". Kenneth was born on the Island of Iona. The picts had been named by the Romans who referred to the highlanders, known to be fierce warriors, as Picti or painted men because of their practice of painting their bodies before going into battle. Alpin won a victory over the picts, who later killed him, and it is said that they displayed his severed head in their camp.

Shortly after his father's death Kenneth became the new clan chieftain and occupied the Pictish strongholds of Fortriu and Forteviot in Perthshire. Following victory Kenneth became accepted as the King of the Picts. He was later made King of the Scots at the talking stone, "Stone of Scone". Kenneth MacAlpin, the first King of Scotland, ruled Scotland for 17 years until his death in 858 AD and his two sons were subsequent Kings of Scotland. In Scotland Mac and McC on the front of a last name means "son of". One of MacAlpin' s daughters later married an Irish King. As the years passed until the battle of Culloden in 1746 clan MacAlpin drifted again into the mist of Celtic history and the clan and the territory, as well as the name, dissipated into many similar, but different spellings and locations. Kings came and went in Scotland, but unfortunately it was often as a result of killing a prior King or his linage. Through the marriage of the Scottish and English linage of the Stuart line the entire British Kingdom was eventually fragilely united.

THE MCCALEB BROTHERS

The looming barbarous Battle of Culloden and it savage and barbaric aftermath imposed on the common folks and clansmen was to have a lasting impact on Scotland and the feudal clan system. The chieftain tribal system would be forever changed and would be the catalyst that encouraged those who could afford escape to do so. Living in the Highlands, were my ancestors, remnants of Clan MacAlpin with one of the variant surname spellings who participated in the recently completed battles and the ominous one to come. William Mccaleb was a Sept of the MacDonnell of Keppoch Clan of Scotland.   T h e Mccaleb family consisted of the father William Mccaleb born in 1695 in Lock Aber, Scotland who later died in the Battle of Prestonpans at age 50. He was married to Mary MacDonnell who was the daughter of the Chief of the MacDonnell Clan. After the father's death the eldest son William Neil became the head of the family. The remaining family consisted of four sons and their ages at the time of the Battle of Culloden were: William Neil Mccaleb age 30, James Mccaleb age 25, John Mccaleb age 23, and Enos Mccaleb age 10. All of the male family members, but young Enos, participated in most of Prince Charles' battles. After watching the death of their father at Prestonpans I am sure it was difficult to continue on.

The most powerful of all the highlands clans was the MacDonnell Clan with more than 100 or more septs within the great clan. Clans were made up of those who were related to the chief and to each other by strong ties of either blood or loyalty. This powerful clan came to the aide of Prince Charles in full force, but other lowland clans stayed loyal to the King.

The McCalebs were noted Jacobites and Scotland was no place for them in the terrible times following the Rising of Forty Five. Fortunately they had laid up cash resources and were in a position to elude the vengeance of the Hanovarian Government. The first step in their escape, as to collect Enos and John's family and get to Dublin. Ireland was more than sympathetic to the Jacobite cause. They crossed at night from Campbeltown to Ballycastle.

paying dearly for the privilege and sharing a dirty berth on a fishing lugger with some other. silent travelers. There. Williams intended. Sara McAlpin, joined the four brothers. She and William were married in the rites of the Catholic Church. There was a dowry went with Sara for she was the daughter of the chief of a Clan McAlpin Sept.

Dublin was a busy seaport. There was a lot of commerce westward to the Carolinas. In tact. The Argyll Colony had been established in I 739 in the Cape Fear Valley of North Carolina. This developed into the largest settlement of Scottish Highlanders anywhere outside Scotland. They decided to go there.

In the spring of 1747 the McCaleb family, Willian1 and Sara. the limping James. John and his family and young Enos sailed aboard the 300-ton ship Duh/in Lass bound for Cape Fear via the Azores. The ship was a merchant vessel. The hold had been very roughly partitioned to provide the semblance of privacy for the immigrants crammed therein. Duh/in Lass was overloaded with 320 passengers and a crew of 35. Many of those sailing had indentured themselves to North Carolina planters or farmers in order to pay the cost of the voyage. In addition, there were stores and personal possessions. Live poultry, pigs and sheep to provide fresh meat were penned in an extended section of the poop deck Many of the passengers were proscribed Jacobites and liable.

To arrest if caught by the government. in the shape of the Kings Royal Navy. The ship's captain Lian, Cooney. had thirty years sailing behind him and some portion of that experience was in dodging navy patrols. So, the ship sailed. grossly: overloaded but with a competent and wily master.

South through Saint George's Channel, across the Celtic Sea leaving the most westerly point of England. Land's End, well on the Port beam and so into the Atlantic. Went *Dublin Lass*.

The weather was kind at this time, although there were many on board who sis no think so. The overcrowding was a hardship from the beginning of the voyage, even to people used to cramped crofts. The captain was not cruel but a practical man of business. He had to make a profit for the owners. The food was staple: oatmeal, potatoes, bread and salted beef or pork with small beer or water. John McCaleb's infant son did not do well on it. Fortunately, they had thought to provide themselves with extra rations for the trip and this eased their conditions. It took thirteen days for the *Dublin Lass* to reach Azores. They dropped anchor in the little harbor of Ponta Delgada, the capital on the Island of Sao Miguel. They took abroad water and some fruit, chickens and lambs. At this time a minor dilemma arose. Two families of Scottish immigrants had enough of voyaging. They wanted to stay there rather than face the terrors of the long haul west into the prevailing winds. Captain Cooney was not eager to refund any of their passage money and at the first the Portuguese authorities were not inclined to accept these newcomers. Tempers rose as they argued. Finally, the Governor relented and they were accepted. Cooney did not relent however, and they received no refund. So, they sailed after two days and left ten Scots men and women to intermingle with the natives.

The North Atlantic was an unkind place even in the springtime. The ship was butting into the wind most of the time. sailing close hauled and pitching quite badly. Still seriously overcrowded and now with almost all the passengers seasick. she became a foul and miserable craft. Ten days out front the Azores the first death occurred. Weakened by lack of nourishment. racked by constant vomiting they succumbed— beginning with the very young and the old. John McCaleb's baby was taken. The Captain said a prayer (there was no priest or minister on board) and they tipped the pathetic little bundle into the seething sea. More passengers were to follow as they struggled on westward. The voyage seemed endless. Squalls of rain added to the spray leaking through the decks and showering the people cramped and miserable below. The McCaleb brothers started to assist the sailors·. The work kept them from dwelling on their tribulation and Captain Cooney was grateful for free labor. Thirty days out from the Azores and forty-five after leaving Dublin. Captain Cooney had to reduce the rations. He had discovered that several barrels of salt beef were inedible. This was a hardship regularly faced by ship's captains. Likely the beef had been sold already rotten in the barrels a favorite ploy of crooked chandlers. Even those able to hold food down were now assailed by hunger. Dysentery beset them and the death rate increased. One positive aspect of the rain was the fact they could collect the rainwater, for drinking water was rationed too. Many of the weary passengers vented their frustrations by complaints to the crew and mates. It was only human nature to seek a convenient scapegoat. Captain Cooney's years at sea had taught him the value of patience. He did what he could to assure them that they were on course and making the best time possible in the circumstances. As some became heated, he had to remind the1n that they had all been warned of the hazards of an ocean voyage before they left Dublin. He and his two mates started to serve their watches with pistols in their belts. The atmosphere was brittle with tension. And then on the fifty-seventh day, out of the Azores and seventy-two from leaving Dublin came the blessed cry from the look out. "Land Ho!" The relief was universal among passengers and crew alike. However, another day was taken up in crushing along the coast and up the long twisting Cape Fear River before the *Dublin Lass* could finally berth in Wilmington, North Carolina. The voyage had lasted seventy-three days and fifty-six had died on the journey.

OKLAHOMA RANCH AND THE GREAT DEPRESSION (1929)

In the early 1900's, William McCalip the eldest and John McCalip his younger brother, the two sons of Pollie and William McCaleb, moved on to 754 acres in Indian Territory that had been purchased by the older brother. Lizzie McCalip Dean their sister had already married and was on her own with her new husband. It was at this time in 1904 that John Wesley McCalip, my grandfather, married Arzella Williams in the Southern Methodist Episcopal Church by Local Elder J. A. Smith in the Cherokee Nation. Family religious beliefs, as with many emigrant groups, had changed through the ages from staunch Roman Catholics in Scotland to different divergent groups in America.

It was here on the ranch land that the two brothers prospered until the arrival of the great depression and the mid-western dust bowel period leading into 1929. William had a total of seven children and John had six children including my father John W. McCalip, Jr. These large farm families were still typical to help with farming and animal rising in the mid-west at this time. My grandfather made extra money as a bronc buster and eventually died from complication from a fall from a horse

Times were hard on the farm and ranch when my father reached his late teens, he appeared to have inherited that western wanderlust, and decided to strike out on his own with very little money and traveling as a free loader on the nearest railroad line to the "pot of gold" in the sunshine state of California. After reaching the Central Coast of California he found work in the oil fields, working on the coastal rail line, and finally with the Union Sugar Plant in the Santa Maria Valley. It was here that his farm skills came in handy with the agricultural department of the plant. At that time in history sugar beets were brought from the fields in wagons drawn by mules and so his farm experience came in handy since he knew animals. He was not afraid of hard work and as the years past he worked his way up to a plant foreman and eventually in later years to an assistant superintendent. With breaks only for military service and to return to the mid-west to marry my mother this became his life's profession. He was a hard worker and he stuck with it!

TENACITY SHOULD BE MY GUIDE

This careful review in my somewhat feverish mind of my distant ancestors and their trials and tribulations as they moved westward was actually quite cathartic in helping make a decision as to my future plans in education and at Casmalia. Tenacity was the trait that was common in all the major events that confronted these earlier ancestors and it came to me that tenacity should be my guide. My fever broke before my wife returned home from her activities and as I lay in bed with tenacity as my guiding light, I again knew that I should not desert my students and community. After all, I was in teaching for the challenge of helping others and these folks and students certainly still needed help. It was my hope that I could deliver. The following Monday morning I catted the County Personnel Office to let the office manager know that I was withdrawing my name from consideration for the "pie in the sky" job at Gaviota School District!

How wise my decision turned out to be because by Thursday of that week I received a call from an eager young investigative reporter for a Santa Barbara County newspaper. Her specialty was running stories that no one else knew about. Somehow the investigative reporter, with a good lead, knew of my attempt to change jobs, so it was extremely important as to how I handled this phone conversation. Notoriety and speaking out continuously, which was good for the community, had certainly changed my life and peoples' expectations of me!

To handle this phone call, I readily admitted to her that I had seriously thought of changing administrative positions to a safer environment because of my personal health concerns, but that this option was out of the question. I was in this for the long run with my students and parents. You would not see me deserting the ship! I also indicated to her that I firmly believed that our efforts would eventually result in the site being "Closed, capped and cleaned up". I went on to tell her that I would be using each and every second of spare time working toward these goals and that I would not rest until this was accomplished. I invited her to call me again when she heard that we had reached our goals and I would be happy to give her another personal interview! Thus, I am sure I will be talking to you again. It was my hope that Kenneth Hunter and his new wife would read this positive and optimistic news story between their court appearances in San Diego.

CHAPTER 13

DECISION HELD IN LIMBO

MOST COUNTY SUPERVISORS ON BOARD

The next six months were limbo months as the whole county waited for a decision from the state health department and Dr. Kizer, but busy ones for our community's attorneys. Many politicians now tried to jump aboard the anti-dump effort as public support for our efforts grew and grew. The supervisors were able to wrangle $475,000 out of Casmalia Resources to cover an air study to be done by Weston Laboratories from Stockton, California. To start off with, a traveling van would be used to sample air and later permanent monitors would be placed in strategic locations and air monitoring would be staggered during 12-hour periods each day.

The Santa Barbara County Grand Jury, on July 2, 1986, issued it final year-end report echoing earlier preliminary reports stating that, "Casmalia Resources should be closed until all health problems are resolved and that the site is a real, present, immediate and substantial endangerment to public health." On July 11th Supervisor Holmdahl, as usual unable to read the writing on the wall, flayed the Grand Jury Report in his usual defense of his good friend from Montecito. Speaking at the Vandenberg Inn in Santa Maria, he cited the executive officer of the local water board as saying, "Ground water is moving southerly, away from the Santa Maria basin". These are the same two yokels that tried to convince us earlier that no water at all existed under the site and a magical impermeable shield existed under the site. All of this while extremely toxic waste sat in unlined lagoons all over the site.

Shortly after Supervisor Holmdahl's simple-minded presentation in Santa Maria, the Environmental Protection Agency personnel briefed the supervisors on July 22nd of earlier testing by the agency assuring the board that they were following up with tough monitoring efforts after three toxic compounds were found in wells around the site. Mr. Filippine of the EPA said, "There are no acceptable standards of contamination for these materials, as any level is unacceptable. Casmalia was not following, at the time of the investigation in 1985, an adequate plan or appropriate field procedures for groundwater sampling and analysis." Supervisor Miyoshi spoke up and noted that the Regional Water Quality Control Board, "…has for years said there is no groundwater under the site", and asked Filippine about it. He diplomatically replied, "It shows how our standards and technology have evolved." I thought when I heard this: How in the hell has drilling a well and taking samples changed in the last few years? A diplomatic response, but certainly outlandish!

On Aug 1st Supervisor Holmdahl tried to pump up his own, "down in the mud" image on the Casmalia Toxic Dump issues in a news release by puffing up the fact that his office was available to help with a new fund the state had to help with a new Hazardous Substance Compensation Program. His office would help anyone who wanted to apply for compensation. County Health pooh-poohed the effort by saying they could give information and data on air and water samples but could not provide proof that the hazardous materials came from Casmalia Toxic Dump. Thus, no one could meet the application requirements. So, in the same news story, it went nowhere! Sometimes I wondered if Holmdahl was playing with a full deck!

Local Congressman (R) Bob Lagomarsino requested an investigation by contacting EPA administrator Lee Thomas and reported in his news release positive results. He stated, "Questions still remain about the geology and hydrology of the site, and their impact on public health and the environment". The congressman also said, "Thomas admitted that the EPA had been remiss in not requiring effective monitoring at the site. But that the EPA will not try to override state enforcement efforts." Lagomarsino's meeting with Thomas came after release early that month of an EPA report which said contaminants were found in a dozen wells used to monitor groundwater around Casmalia Resources.

Then again, on Nov. 19,1986, Largomarsino's office announced, "...The EPA is sending a top-flight investigative team based in Denver that had been assigned to Casmalia. The NEIC team has been described as a super sleuth investigative unit. It is comprised of top EPA members from throughout the country." He requested the team after several meetings with EPA administrator Lee Thomas after there were, "Conflicting reports about the facility from various government agencies and concern expressed by local residents regarding potential health hazards." Casmalia residents appreciated his efforts, but still actions moved slowly.

On Aug. 15th the State Assembly Office of Research released a 96-page report at the request of Assemblywoman Lucy Killes, the chairwoman, of the Assembly Committee on Alternative Technologies. The report, she said, was titled, "Today's Toxic Dump Sites: Tomorrow's Toxic Cleanup Sites." The report was devastating for Kenneth Hunter and Casmalia Resources and tore apart the fallacies of his scheme for the world to see. The report disputes previous statements by Casmalia Resources' owners that no groundwater existed below the site. Instead, the report cites, "...an EPA report which says there is groundwater from about 150 feet to 200 feet below the surface in the north part of the facility. At lower elevations in the southern part, groundwater is no deeper than 10 to 100 feet below the surface."

In addition, the Regional Water Quality Control Board inspections last April revealed possible violations such as liquids found seeping through containment dikes below four ponds. Two of those seeps had "measurable flow". A second possible violation occurred after deep excavation of the pesticide/solvent landfill revealed a substantial amount of water. It could not be determined if the water was collected runoff or groundwater. Class I dumps must have underground permeability not exceeding one inch per year. The report noted that in May 1985 the Regional Water Quality Control Board reported that, "…fractured soils at Casmalia Resources near surface impoundments have the potential for vertical and horizontal movement of constituents". Correspondence between Water Board officials last March says that, "…the permeabilities at the Casmalia Disposal site were faster than permitted by law-300 times faster in some cases." A geologist for the board is quoted as saying, " There are no monitoring wells at Casmalia Resources that can immediately detect leakage from containment structures." It was a damning report and I wondered why action had not been taken by front line regulators? Actions that should have been taken years ago were lacking. How did Hunter manage to manipulate these inspectors to keep his scheme moving forward as did Ponzi in Boston and Dominelli in San Diego? Each day the dump site went unchecked, the money kept rolling through the front gate and I began to wonder where some of it might have been going?

STATE DITHERING ON DECISION

At the next supervisors' meeting Dr. Hart, again, noted the bomb threat at Lakeview School that disrupted the state's June 12 hearing and stated, "it proved that some residents were in a rage while the whole community distrusted government agencies." He then brought up the issue of relocating residents. I am sure he was right about the rage, but I also knew he must be aware that he was the main player in creating that rage and distrust of government agencies. Thus, the concern he expressed I still felt was, in effect, concern for his own future personal safety. He indicated to the board that the state had told him they would release the findings at the end of the month.

At the meeting he recommended the board support closure as a way of forcing the state to act and to reassure the public. But Chairman David Yager criticized the state for, "…dithering on this endlessly". The board agreed that it was too early to seek closure and unanimously voted to send a letter to the state asking it to release the findings of the report. Miyoshi said, "The letter should be a strong statement. I still get complaints of odors, but mostly residents call me to vent their frustration about waiting for action. The six-month delay indicates indifference on the part of the state." Dr. Hart then stated, "I can't get information because, in a sense we're in an adversarial position with the state. The county's concern is the health and safety of its residents, but the state has another responsibility-ensuring there's a site that can receive the most dangerous toxic waste.

How true Dr. Hart was in his statement. But, why should this agency, with an obvious conflict of interest, be making a decision about people's health and safety?

NEW YEAR AND A COURT DECISION

As 1986 passed and 1987 rolled in, several events emerged as a mouse that later sounded much more like a lion. Unnoticed by myself and others, these events seemed rather routine and mundane, but were extremely significant. We were now moving into the new year with seven months and still no "501" decision by the state health department!

The first of these events was the appointment in January of James Ryerson as the new Air Pollution Control District Director. This department was merely a subdivision of the county health department, but major changes in the organization of this department were in the works to be brought about by events that were to unfold as the year developed. At this point in time the real head of the department was Dr. Hart, who was the head of the entire health department. It was with him that the buck and responsibility stopped. I watched the news continuously on these subjects and I was unaware of Ryerson's appointment

The second of these events was a court battle in far-off Los Angeles with the state over the subpoena for the medical data of Casmalia residents and plaintiffs in the $1 billion law suit against Casmalia Resources. State health officials wanted access to results of medical tests conducted earlier that year on 167 Casmalia residents. The medical study was done at the expense of the team of attorneys representing the community. State officials had been trying for several months to obtain the medical data. In September, a state subpoena for the records was served on Robert Sulnick, one of our attorneys, in Los Angeles, but he refused to release the information without a court order and this triggered the court hearing on Jan. 8th. Our legal team, Toxey Hall Smith, Robert Sulnick and Richard Brenneman, vigorously opposed the state's efforts with a 40-page brief, declaration, and exhibits showing that the state could have done their own testing years ago and did not. The entire community helped by signing a "Joint Declaration of Casmalia Residents" in a short span of time. In our legal team's opinion, the declarations were pivotal and highly effective in communicating to the court the community's feelings and intentions against the State and the dump site owner.

At the hearing Mr. Sulnick, who had become a good friend in the course of the dump struggle, argued brilliantly. He started off by stating, "forcing the release of the records would violate my clients' right to privacy, and the physician-patient privilege. If the state wanted the results so badly, it should have gained the community's good will, and should have funded its own study."

Sulnick and the others representing the townspeople had resisted the state partly because they thought their clients' case could be harmed if the results were release prematurely. Richard Brenneman, another attorney representing the community said, "…the study represents a bargaining chip to trade with the other side. It is important that we protect our clients' interest.

It was also pointed out that, although the state did not have raw data, they had access to the study's summary and statements by the toxicologist who designed the study who said, "… health tests showed significant changes in blood and urine samples taken from Casmalia residents as compared to a control group. All this was available to the state plus tests of four school children at Casmalia School which, early on, showed the same abnormalities." Sulnick added, "…my clients did not think they would have anything to gain by releasing the study to either state or county officials. They don't have much faith in the state or in the county."

At the end of the hearing, Los Angeles County Superior Court Judge Ricardo A. Torres quashed the subpoena and ordered that Sulnick did not have to turn over his clients' medical data to the state Department of Health Services. He agreed that it was privileged evidence in their lawsuit against the dump site owner. Now that the state was denied access there was speculation that state health officials would release a decision on the 501 hearing held last June. Dr. Kizer had told reporters at the 501 hearing that the results would be released by the end of summer, but that time line had come and gone and the people in Casmalia were still trapped!

SAFE AND ALL CLEAR

Speculation and anticipation was running high in Santa Barbara County when state health officials again estimated the target date of January 26[tn] for the release of the report. They blamed the delay on the great amount of testimony which made preparation major, major work. They also could not verify if Dr. Kizer would appear before the board of supervisors with the results. They should have asked me, as I knew from the arrogant letters in my file there was not a chance he would even be near Santa

Barbara County when the results were released. Good old-fashioned tarred and feathered came to mind when I watched this report on TV!

Supervisor Toru Miyoshi said, "I am disappointed at the belated date of the report, but I am optimistic with a degree of reservation. I am hoping that the issue of public health and safety will not be compromised for political expediency."

The results of all clear, it's safe, and no closure were devastating for the town folks in Casmalia, but we needed to press on with our goals to "close it, cap it and clean it up". At least I was prepared in advance for the negative outcome because of the advanced warning in my files. The reaction of the two supervisors with districts impacted by the dump the most were very interesting. Toru Miyoshi, our main supporter, called it like he saw it and expressed displeasure by saying of the results, "Very ludicrous and political expediency at its worst". This said it all.

Holmdahl was a strong supporter of the Casmalia Toxic Dump and had only changed and modified his vote and public statements because of public pressure moving away from his earlier positions. Holmdahl's reaction to the news was toned down somewhat because he knew that the public's approval rating was now 80% in favor of the community of Casmalia, but his response to the news still made me nauseated. He started off by saying that in wake of the DHS decision he would continue to press state officials for compensation for Casmalia property owners. He said, "The multitude of publicity about the alleged health problems has so lowered property values in the town that the state is still obligated to buy up the town of Casmalia." So, according to DeWayne, it was just publicity that was the problem, not the toxic dump site. He then went on to give himself a pat on the back saying, "Even though it was not closed the facility has greatly scaled back operation from 1984 levels. That includes an agreement between the dump and the county which trimmed truck traffic from about 130 per day to about 35. It's a large victory compared to what we were at." Community desperation was now at an all-time high!

PART THREE: THE END GAME AND MORE PUSH

CHAPTER 14

ZIMPRO CYANIDE TRUTH AND KIZER PICKET

POST "501" WORKSHOPS

State Health Services officials planned to try to explain Dr. Kizer's decision to not close Casmalia Resources in a series of three schedules workshops. It turned out to be harder to face locals than I am sure they had anticipated. Each workshop became progressively more heated as they progressed. The workshops were designed to explain the decision and lay out their plans for monitoring the ongoing operations of the dump site.

Angelo Bellomo, a state health employee, was given the unpleasant task of explaining to an angry crowd, his department's efforts to monitor groundwater. He conceded that contamination in the water directly below the surface ponds had been detected. He tried to assure everyone that if contamination migrated, "…it would do so at a rate of only a few feet per year and he added that extraction wells could be sunk to pull contaminated water out of the ground and that this is a common process for sites that are leaking. He went on to say that early detection is important and critical and that they were going to upgrade the monitoring system and that this would take about 18 months." The 18 months portion of his presentation did not sound urgent and did not go over well with the assembled group.

He also went on to explain to the group that the state had $50,000 available to set up a group of citizens as an advisory group and also that the County of Santa Barbara still had the option of closing down the facility with a public nuisance suit, but they would have to convince a court of law that the nuisance existed. At this point that is just what Dr. Hart intended to accomplish.

Dr. Hart stated again, "County and state health officials have lost credibility with residents living near the dump, it should not reopen until health officials can restore some credibility to the process, he suspects that there was offsite migration." Amen, Dr. Hart, as it sounded like he had seen the light!

Former resident Lew Dunn spoke up next and said, "Anyone who believes there is no such migration is naive and that every toxic waste dump site in the country has leaked at one time or another and it is going to happen here." Jerry Corlew spoke up and said, "These meeting are just to wear down dump opponents to lessen their advocacy for closure and I'm sickened by you people, I really am." Toward the end of the meeting a woman wearing a yellow Parents Against Casmalia T-shirt stood up in the back of the room and yelled, "We don't believe you." After this outburst Bellomo closed the meeting by saying, "the 501 hearing doesn't mean we've closed all the doors as we are ready to look at facts and reconsider it." Thus, the first angry meeting came to a close and had some minor impact on state officials when they were on the hot seat, but very little!

The final two workshops were much like the first and the credibility gap between opponents of Casmalia Resources and the state Department of Health Services did not narrow in these later quarrelsome meetings. The next meeting included not only personnel from the state Department of Health Service, but also from the state Air Resources Board and the

Air Pollution Control District from Santa Barbara County. On several occasions during these meetings officials were accused of impropriety in the way they handled the dump. Jerry Barca from Los Alamos who owned ranch property close to Casmalia said to the panel in not so uncertain terms, "You guys have got to get off Mr. Hunter's payroll." Angelo Bellomo of the DHS shot back, "I certainly take exception to that suggestion."

Barca and his wife, Cathy, also showed a video tape of television news reports depicting toxic filled barrels being buried at the facility without lids. After the presentation Bellomo said, "There is no restriction to burying barrels without lids. Lids on containers only provide a false sense of security; Security that instead should be placed on the integrity of the site itself. It is not suggesting anything inappropriate is going on at the facility." Cathy shot back in an angry voice, " Apparently you have not read the 96-page report from the State Assembly that devastatingly tore apart the integrity of the site with water under the site and leaking ponds that reach 300 times faster than the legal limit permitted at dump sites with no action by regulators such as yourself." Her comment received massive applause from those in attendance.

Lew Dunn, formerly of Casmalia, also spoke up at one of these meetings saying, "One air study indicated that the amount of benzene in air sampled at Casmalia School in December of 1984 was higher than the amount recorded in Los Angeles during the worst air pollution day between 1977 and 1982." Dr. Kelter on the panel responded to Dunn saying, "These exposure numbers are extremely small and these levels would be the same as running your auto in an enclosed garage." Dunn shot back, noticeable agitated, in a loud voice, "What about the hundreds of other compounds in the air those days that added to the mix? What about the small school children who could not get enough oxygen to breathe the day our school was forced to close because of the mix of toxins in the air? Where were you, you so called regulators, when the community needed you the most? Dr. Kelter had no response to this emotional outpouring of heated questions.

Richard Brenneman, one of several attorneys representing both the Casmalia School District and the citizens of Casmalia in the multimillion lawsuit against the facility, also had a lengthy and heated exchange with Bellomo, Kelter, and Dave Willis on the panel. Brenneman pointed out that "as a matter of law, complaints of health problems linked to Casmalia Resource was legally admissible evidence along with the health summary that was provided to the state". He asked, "Why was this not given appropriate weight in the "501" decision?" The give and take at all these meetings were hostile and negative as the public, and the folks in Casmalia and Orcutt in particular, were fed up with Dr. Kizer and company.

But, in addition to the rancor, two positive items developed from these meetings and this time period. First, was the citizen advisory group which the folks from Casmalia including myself jumped right on and became members who met periodically. The $50,000 from the state could be used to fund our own technical advisor. This we used to engage the services of a young professor from the University of California at Santa Barbara. He was later tasked to tell us if the Zimpro process had any merit to dispose of toxic waste or was it just a sham. Later down the road his scientifically researched answered, as we all suspected, it was a "sham" used to keep the scheme going and the money flowing into the front gate. Second, during this same time period the University of California at Santa Barbara entered the Casmalia fray with the offer of a bargain price to the County Board of Supervisors to do an ecological study of the dump and surroundings, "It was to determine the actual and potential environmental effects of the Casmalia facility or to develop a monitoring system to detect such effects in the future." The study would include investigating toxic effects on animals and plants in a wide circle around the site, and sample blood tissue of domestic cattle and wild animals. All normal University grant overhead for research would be waived because of this projects, significance and importance to the community of Casmalia. The study was offered by Dr. Daniel Botkin, professor of biology and environmental studies, and would also include experts in environmental geology and geography.

Graduate and undergraduate students would also contribute. Years later, when completed, there was a dead zone around the dump site. I noticed after this proposal, which I had not paid attention to before, that we no longer had birds chirping and flying around the school building. This study confirmed these observations.

DR. KIZER PICKETED IN SAN LUIS OBISPO

It was fairly warm Wednesday morning at work when Meg, the school secretary, interrupted me in class for what she termed an important and urgent phone call. When I got to the phone in the adjacent Principal's office, I found out that it was a close friend of mine who lived in San Luis Obispo and who had noticed that Dr. Kizer was set to speak to the San Luis Obispo Medical Society that night at their regular meeting to be held at Park Suite Hotel. Kizer was foolishly honoring a long-standing invitation from the San Luis Obispo County Medical Society to discuss state health programs. His visit gave us a foot in the door for a protest and bad publicity for him. The call made my day and was a perfect opportunity for us to express our anger directly to the director and not to mere underlings. I quickly made calls to Nick, Jerry and Kenneth and suggested we needed to protest at his speaking engagement that evening and then Meg and I started down my phone list of media groups to let them know of the planned picket event. So, the word went out and a small group of us prepared for the evening drive up the coast to the neighboring city. I finally could put my new megaphone to work. It was the latest model and I am sure they would be able to hear us inside the building as well as doctors who arrived at the building. I was giddy with anticipation! Surpassing Dr. Hart- Dr. Kizer was another person I would enjoy having a few words with in my private office. But I planned to keep it professional because many from the community were bringing along their children and my students. Students and parents prepared protest signs that afternoon after school. After checking my batteries, I put my megaphone in my auto for my drive up the coast at the designated departure time. The show was now on the road. It surely would be a great publicity event for the community.

We all arrived early and got organized on the sidewalks out front of the hotel. I suggested that we all keep moving on the side walk so that no one would get arrested. We were in a perfect location as patrons and doctors arriving could hear us easily.

I planned to share the megaphone as I had no desire to keep speaking for any length of time. When the news media started arriving, I immediately went into my one-on-one interview mode. I explained that were here protesting the recent decision of Dr. Kizer to keep the Casmalia Toxic Dump open in northern Santa Barbara County and that he had concluded that the dump did not pose any, "imminent and substantial danger to the community's health and environment" and we strongly disagree.

"Ken Kizer is killing us." Lou Dunn, the former five-year resident said. "I have emphysema. The big question is, Do I smoke? No, I don't smoke. Ken kizer can shut the toxic waste dump down tomorrow just with a phone call. I have been to all the hearings and several protests".

Sixteen-year-old Bill Buck from Righetti High School said, "I started protesting against Casmalia a year ago when I started noticing strange odors at school. I have a lot of friends with health problems, everything from just runny noses and sore throats to serious respiratory problems." One protester's sign read, "No More Lies, Close Casmalia Dump". They were all colorful signs and the picket was a smashing success.

ZIMPRO AND MY CYANIDE VISIT WAS A GAME CHANGER

It had become my practice, and some would say my obsession, to periodically visit two specific governmental agencies to go through public records. I knew my rights under the Freedom of Information laws. These visits would range between one to three days at a time. I felt that I would eventually find some useful information, but on most occasions I did not and it was disappointing. Still yet, I kept my practice up with high expectations. I always called first to make an appointment rather than arriving unannounced. I usually greeted them with a teasing joke about myself. I had even got to know the personnel at these offices and they actually greeted me with friendship and courtesy as well as providing me with a private area to work. On this particular day in March of 1987, I was visiting the Santa Barbara Office of the County Air Pollution Control District. This was not to be a day like other visits and this was a day that would answer many of the questions that nagged me about my closure of the school and the departure of the old air pollution director, John English, from the department. It would be a day that would change the course of events for the continuing confrontations with the dump site, the county, and the state.

When I first sat down at my assigned location and started poring through records, I noticed something out of the ordinary. Many of the pages were tagged with yellow stick-on notes that acted as a flag to those particular items. At first, I just ignored these and started at the beginning of the file and worked laboriously through it looking at each page. I finally reached a flagged record page and began to read it. It was then I realized the importance of these. None of these had been in the public record on my earlier visits. The items were shocking to say the least!

The first one detailed the fact that the Zimpro Unit had a one-year permit to construct, but never received a permit to operate. It had been operating without permits for years. The next one detailed April 10, 1984 memo to then director John English from engineer Philip which summarized a meeting with a panel of experts. According to Philip, Dr. Richad March of Allan Hancock College expressed, "Concern that untreatable material was being injected into the unit and this was causing a localized serious problem". Dr. Harold Cota of Cal Poly in San Luis Obispo Expressed, "safety concerns for persons who work at the site and for neighbors." The panel of experts recommended jointly, "Testing surrounding air for toxics and a system for automatically shutting down the unit when toxics reached unsafe levels." Later, as I dug through the tagged records, I found confirmed overruns of steamed Cyanide gas on the days prior to, during, and after I was forced to close my small school in 1984. Those that know anything about law knew that this was the smoking gun for the county's own liability. Shocked was putting it mildly, as I now knew the secret that the old director had hidden the day of the confrontation in my principal's office. He knew it was highly toxic Cyanide gas mixed in with other highly toxic materials. He knew it was unsafe in the area and he had done nothing to prevent the event and protect small school children. He also sat like a lump on a log at the task force meeting and said nothing before we went into my office. Thus, despite the hundreds of over runs, the system kept spewing toxic steam into the air and the scam continued with regulators looking the other way as millions of dollars came through the front gate. All this despite warnings from the panel of experts!

The new Air Pollution Control Director James Ryerson, who came on board in January, was put on notice of the problems in a memo from inspector John Carroll on Feb. 13, 1987 which outlined the overruns that topped 320 parts per million many times for 24 hours per day. The question now became what would he do about the problem and the lack of a permit? I also asked one of the office personnel where all these documents had been since I had never had seen them in my earlier visits but they were now tagged and in the public file. She hesitantly said, " They are tucked away in the vacant desk of the departed director for all these years. He always kept control of them." I said to myself, "I bet he did!" It took me a full three days to finish my quest for information, even with tagged files, as I now did not want to miss any items of information.

Because of these document claims were eventually filled against Santa Barbara County and the State of California for a total of $1.4 billion for careless and negligent supervision of Casmalia Resources toxic dump site by 361 plaintiffs in June of 1987. Since it began operations in 1972 the question of which government level, county, state, or federal government held responsibility for enforcing the safety rules remains clouded. County officers listed as specific defendants included former APCD inspector John R. Carroll, who now worked for Casmalia Resources; K. George Philip, former APCD engineering supervisor;

and John B. English, former APCD director. Attorney Robert Sulnick said, "Dr. Lawrence Hart is automatically included since he is the overall supervisor of the health department which includes the APCD." It seemed appropriate that these county folks were named and this gave me great pleasure for the many long days I had spent plowing through government records and negatively dealing with these specific individuals in the community of Casmalia. All, except Dr. Hart, were now gone from county service.

But before this law suit was filled the new director had some important decisions to make. After I made the disclosures at a news conference of the lack of permits and violations, Toro Miyoshi followed up with his own news conference and unfortunately Mr. Ryerson at the same time announced that the Zimpro Unit was being operated in "substantial conformity" with conditions set forth in the 1982 permit to construct. On April 21 1987 Ryerson did an about face, I am sure from pressure from most of the supervisors, and stated he did, "... a more detailed and careful review of the record and this had resulted in the discovery of numerous violations". County officials said that my efforts expedited the issue, but they would have discovered the violations themselves. Doubtful, since this failure to regulate had gone on for five years or more while school children were chased out of their school building.

Ryerson ordered the shutdown of the Zimpro Unit, "... until they can show they can operate it safely." Mr. Ryerson did this and denied the permit to operate he said, "... it is within my authority over air pollution which is separate from the state's ability to regulate toxic dumps." In addition, the county, separate from the air pollution district's action, now moved forward with other efforts to curtail the toxic dump after a request to the state with virtually no response.

The issue facing the board of supervisors at their regular April meeting was an urgency ordinance prepared by deputy county counsel Jed Beebe that would require extensive groundwater and air monitoring around Casmalia. If owners can't meet a deadline of July 20 to accomplish the monitoring, after an appeal process, the ordinance gives the county power to ask the courts for a temporary closure or fines up to $25,000 per day for each violation. Beebe warned the supervisors that if they pass it, the state may challenge it in court. He further said, "…because it is an urgency ordinance it requires a vote of four supervisors rather than the usual majority of three." The vote was 4 to 0 with one supervisor absent.

Supervisor Bill Wallance, the chairman, started the meeting off by saying, "It's time to put a little caution aside. We simply cannot continue to tolerate the community's problems. Those include numerous health complaints, reduction in property values and fear of contamination that reached nationwide attention through Time Magazine, among others. It's time for action."

Before the hearing many residents joined a picket in front of the county building that had been organized by Greenpeace, the international environmentalist organization helping us. I used my opportunity to speak to say, "I was grateful for the support of Greenpeace, my students are ill all the time with respiratory problems. Dump fumes are bad two or three times a week. It is not a safe place to live." Protestors lined the supervisors hearing room with posters that said, "Close it, cap it, clean it up." Fighting back tears, one mother said that their children were suffering eye irritation and respiratory problems. Pat Gourley told the board, "A lot of us have never broken a law in our lives and we're feeling that we're going to have to. By being nice, nothing seems to get done. Please help us!"

Ken Hunter was visibly upset by the audience response when he was speaking when he said, " The board is responding to scare tactics and a temporary closure of the site means a permanent closure". The chamber erupted into applause and a standing ovation. He looked dumbfounded and that ended his presentation. At last, the community, through perseverance, had achieved a small victory and reward for all their efforts. It was one small step but a well-deserved one!

CHAPTER 15

THE JED BEEBE WARNING

COUNTY LEGAL ACTIONS

The community of Casmalia was ecstatic to see the County of Santa Barbara finally taking some action, but the odds seemed to be stacked against local control of toxic dumps in California by various state laws that gave close to exclusive jurisdiction to the state Health Department and in particular to the State Health Director. It was also great to see the new APCD director doing the right thing and taking a firm stand. They were at last making an effort to protect public health and standing up against the state and the dump site scam. Young Deputy County Counsel Jed Beebe had, right up front, warned all the supervisors, "Expect challenges in court on the urgency ordinance." This prediction turned out to be an accurate educated guess of events to unfold. But no one, I am sure, expected the large volume of litigation that was to come. Jed turned out to be just the right man for the job and I am sure he did not realize at the time he would be pushing the legal issues to higher and higher courts.

Dr. Hart wasted no time in the implementation of the new ordinance. Chairman Bill Wallace said, "It will clearly lead us to court. We're trying to find a legal way to close the dump temporarily." The new law was seen

115

as a test of local authority over the dump, (as Casmalia Resources) now handled virtually all of Southern California's hazardous wastes. The new ordinance allowed the county health director to specify the number and location of air and ground water testing devices for Casmalia by June 1. The testing system must be in place by July 20. Casmaila Resources officials are given the right to appeal the health director's plan to the Board of Supervisors. Violation of the new law could bring a $25,000 daily fine and ultimately a Superior Court closure order. It was a no-nonsense effort by county government. Both Dr. Hart and Mr. Ryerson moved forward with their two separate long overdue regulatory moves.

Kenneth Hunter immediately requested a hearing in front of the County Board of Supervisors claiming that the time frame is unreasonable and cannot be implemented by the July 20th deadline. The hearing was set for June 22nd in front of the Board of Supervisors. In addition, his attorney submitted a letter from Alex Cunningham, DHS deputy director supporting their position to Mr. Ryerson. Ryerson responded by saying he had ordered the Zimpro Unit closed "…because it was incapable of handling the waste streams. It broke down every two to three days last year because of the volume and concentrations of toxics. So, it couldn't be considered a simple unexpected problem." His decision was an air emission violation and not a toxic issue regulated by the state. The fact that the letter was sent in support of Casmalia Resources by the state pointed out to dump opponents that the state had very few other locations for toxic waste and that the county would have two powerful opponents in court, both the state and the dump. Jed Beebe admitted, "…the state retains the primary authority over toxic waste dumps, but it doesn't preempt reasonable local regulation."

These moves by the county to protect the public were a threat to the ongoing money flow and the scam. Regulators were no longer under his control. In response to this effort, he moved forth both legally, illegally and proposal wise to increase the diminishing capacity of the toxic dump site. First, he started touting a study prepared by Canonie Environmental, a Denver based planning and engineering firm that they started distributing the week of the hearing to the county supervisors and the public. This released plan called for more treatment of hazardous wastes, plus construction of new, triple lined ponds and landfills. It envisioned two new additional Zimpro Wet Air Oxidation Units plus other processing equipment. It also proposed development of a big landfill for non-hazardous trash as well as raising the idea of building a railroad spur to provide an alternative means of transportation of wastes to Casmalia. It both included a short-term plan designed to take the facility through the year 1998 as well as a long- term component through 2030. Within the next few months, they planned on applying for permits to construct new ponds. Oh! How grand these plans were. They, I am sure, made the uninformed jump for joy! Again, it was similar to a Ponzi scheme with positive, well paid attorneys to keep the regulators away, new ideas, public relations outreaches, and anything to keep the flow of money coming through the front gate and eventually moving into his pockets!

As soon as the supervisors decided against Casmalia Resources, its law firm filed a court challenge asking for an injunction. They argued that the county's attempts to accelerate expensive monitoring efforts are preempted by the state and are unreasonable without a finding of imminent danger to the public health and safety. All parties agree that the court's decision will be precedent-setting. Next the county supervisor received a heavy-handed letter Hunter moved forth both legally, illegally and proposal-wise to increase the diminishing capacity of the toxic dump site. First, he started touting a study prepared by Canonie Environmental, a Denver based planning and engineering firm that they started distributing the week of the hearing to the county supervisors and the public. This released plan called for more treatment of hazardous wastes, plus construction of new, triple lined ponds and landfills. It envisioned two new additional Zimpro Wet Air Oxidation Units plus other processing equipment. It also proposed development of a big landfill for non-hazardous trash as well as raising the idea of building a railroad spur to provide an alternative means of transportation of wastes to Casmalia. It both included a short-term plan designed to take the facility through the year 1998 as well as a long- term component through 2030. Within the next few months, they planned on applying for permits to construct new ponds. Oh! How grand these plans were. They, I am sure, made the uninformed jump for joy! Again, it was similar to a Ponzi scheme with positive, well paid attorneys to keep the regulators away, new ideas, public relations outreaches, and anything to keep the flow of money coming through the front gate and eventually moving into his pockets!

As soon as the supervisors decided against Casmalia Resources, its law firm filed a court challenge asking for an injunction. They argued that the county's attempts to accelerate expensive monitoring efforts are preempted by the state and are unreasonable without a finding of imminent danger to the public health and safety. All parties agree that the court's decision will be precedent-setting. Next the county supervisor received a heavy-handed letter from the state saying their activities were a violation of state law. The county counsel's office was reviewing the letter.

In addition to legal action Casmalia Resources was desperate for more room for toxic material, so it illegally started up its sprinklers again to enhance evaporation. On May 23rd Nick Irmiter and former Santa Barbara County Grand Jury Foreman Hugh Hanna photographed on-site spraying which should have stopped in 1985. The photos clearly showed that spraying was continuing. The county was cramping the income and style of Kenneth Hunter and his new wife. I wondered what other illegal activities they would try to keep the cash cow reducing?

The pending legal action, after some court delays, was finally heard on July 17th. Casmalia's resources lost its legal challenge and Superior Court Judge Ronald Stevens denied the company's request for a preliminary injunction that would have prevented the county from enforcing a monitoring ordinance while the suit goes to trial. Stevens said, "… not ruling on the merits of the case, but I see no evidence that the county didn't have authority to pass the ordinance." Casmalia Resources officials decided to appeal the lower court's rejection of the request for an injunction to the three judge Court of Appeals in Ventura.

On Sept. 9th Casmalia Resources announced that it would not reopen its closed Zimpro Unit citing county regulation, restrictions, and costs as the reason. The county had been requesting that the site fund a detailed study to examine the performance and effectiveness of the unit. All of us on the Advisory Group already knew the answer as our technical advisor had already told us that this machine did not have a chance in hell of processing any toxic material successfully using pressure and high temperature, so I am sure this was the underlying reason for the decision. So, the Zimpro Unit was now off the table as an issue at Casmalia Resource. But Casmalia Toxic Dump did have a great monetary year for 86-87, as the firm brought in another $33 million with $3.3 million going the County of Santa Barbara.

Several months later the appellate court in Ventura reached a unanimous decision that again ruled against Casmalia Resources, and indirectly against the State of California, that ended for the moment a dispute about whether the county or the state had exclusive jurisdiction over toxic dumps. They ruled that the county and local jurisdictions could exercise reasonable regulation. Michael Cooney the dump's attorney said, "The owners will present plans as required by the county". Jed Beebe responded, "… so far they have been disputing their obligations under the ordinance. We expect them to be cooperative."

WATER QUALITY BOARD VISIT

Nick and Hugh's discovery of the sprinkler systems illegally in operation, as well as my success in finding information at the APCD, spiked my interest in what they might also be doing in reference to water quality. It was time again for my periodic visit to look at records, under the Freedom of Information Act, at the local state Regional Water Quality Control Board in San Luis Obispo.

I discovered on this visit that our community's efforts, along with other similar communities nationwide who were in similar boats, were slowly beginning to produce results both locally, state wide, and nationally. The state and nation had finally come to the realization that a problem existed with the need to deal with toxic waste properly. However, the results of my visit were both gratifying and worrisome.

Gratifying, because I discovered letters and information that had not been made public in the media that would make good fodder for the news, but that had both good and bad ramifications. In letters written in November and March Kenneth Hunter, in response to the Local Water Board's secret demands, notified the two state agencies that Casmalia Offficials planned to close 21 ponds and five pads and that detailed closure plans were being prepared. There were approximately 40 large ponds and 15 very shallow ponds or pads on the disposal site. Thus, it was about half the site.

At my Friday new conference where I released copies of the letters, Michael Cooney the attorney for Casmalia Resources, responding for Hunter and said that site operators plan to pump the liquid from the ponds, mix it with cement and then bury the solidified material in onsite landfills. One pond is being drained, he said, but none of the waste materials had been buried yet. This sounded par for the course, because the site usually goes ahead with an activity, and then they expect regulators to give it the green light. When I first heard this plan my first question was wouldn't the toxic waste just leach out of the cement? The cleanup had been triggered in part by the state Toxic Pits Cleanup Act, which takes effect in June 1988.

Provisions of the act specify that hazardous waste ponds within a half-mile of a potential drinking water source cannot be used to store liquids after June.

Kenneth Hunter and other dump officials initially claimed there was no drinking water source within a half-mile of the site, but staff members of the state Regional Water Board now disagreed. They pointed out that four water wells were dug on property adjoining the disposal site in 1982 to supply water for showers and restrooms at the facility. The water was pumped from a shallow aquifer in the upper soil. This was the same aquifer that surrounding ranches used for watering cattle and the same water that the school district and community had used in years past prior to it being pumped from the Santa Maria Valley. It was incredible that the Regional Water Board had allowed this dump site to operate in the first place at this location!

Eric Gobler, senior water resource control engineer, responded to my news conference by stating, "We consider the whole site to be within a half-mile of that aquifer. We have advised Casmalia Resources that all the ponds on the site should be closed and not just half of the total." At my news event I pointed out, " We're happy that this is occurring, but it raises a lot of issues. One of the main ones is, what happens if Hunter is unable to meet the closure deadline and just walks away and abandons the site? Is anyone reviewing the proposed closure procedure?" Gobler responded to this question by saying, "The state has not decided what to do if waste disposal sites and other private concerns fail to comply with the provisions of the act. In addition to mandating closure of the ponds, the act also prohibits Casmalia Resources from storing hazardous liquids on site in the future in either lined or unlined ponds. Rainwater could be stored on site, but it would have to be kept in uncontaminated ponds. Storage of rainwater is an important issue because Casmalia Resources is not permitted to dispose of any water off site. In addition to the state deadline, Casmalia Resources is facing a federal act that requires closure of all unlined hazardous liquid waste ponds by November 1988."

Cooney responded, reassuringly saying, "Officials at Casmalia Resource intend to comply with both the state and federal acts. They have been planning for a long time to close all the ponds. Our plan has been to phase out the open ponding of liquids in unlined ponds, and switch to the landfilling of solid wastes. Casmalia will continue to accept hazardous liquids, but the goal of the site is to neutralize them in treatment units."

Just as in the J. David affair, well paid lawyers were making the case to continue the scam even as regulators slowly closed in and took some action. The major plan for the site, released during the year, was a well-orchestrated distraction just as Cooney's performance, both intended to make the public feel that all was under control as well as to snow the regulators. I could see desertion of the dump site on the horizon because the treatment processes were merely a sham! As the money flow dwindled the site would eventually close, but what then?

CONTAMINATES UNDER AND AROUND THE DUMP SITE

In early October, several toxic chemicals were found under the dump site. The chemicals found onsite included carbon tetrachloride, methylene chloride and trichloroethylene commonly known as TCE. These are found most often in solvents. Materials found offsite included cyanide, phenol, pentachlorophenol and toluene. All of these offsite chemicals were found offsite in both ground water and in surface water. This testing was done and submitted as samples as required by proposition 65 approved by voters the prior fall. The proposition requires numerous operators of waste dumps to submit samples of waste assessment tests. The proposition also required state officials to notify county health officials within 72 hours if the discharge "might potentially affect drinking water sources."

The state of course down played the event stating "the contamination represents no immediate health threat." However, we had Dr. Harts attention at the local level and he immediately sent an order Monday which told Casmalia Resources " take immediate action to mitigate the contamination and submit a plan in two weeks for removing all ground water under the site." As usual, Attorney Cooney questioned Hart's authority to issue the order saying "… as we understand it, clean-up of water under the site would be under the jurisdiction of the state Regional Water Board." The Board of Supervisors asked that Bill Leonard, director of the Water Board attend the next meeting to answer board questions.

The executive director of the Water Board was a no-show at the county meeting and this miffed the county supervisors. Supervisor Toru Miyoshi said Leonard's response letter was indicative of the agency's "insensitivity to our concerns." Instead of coming to Santa Barbara he said he would be working with other agencies having regulatory authority over the site to prepare an appropriate response to the limited information. He said the test report findings, "… were not unexpected." Boy! This statement coming from an agency that just a few years ago agreed with the dump owner, "… no water exists under the site and a magical barrier protected everything." He again stated that ground water under the site, "… moves at only a few feet per year and there is time to complete additional testing and take any remedial action required before it reaches the site's edge." Mr. Leonard seemed to be unaware that the recent testing showed it already offsite!

Mr. Leonard then added insult to injury by lecturing the supervises about which agencies were in charge by outlining four different laws and sets of regulations administered by a combination of four state and federal agencies. Although not required to by law, he closed the insulting letter by saying he would, as a courtesy, keep the county informed of any new test results. So, after reading a copy of this letter my question became, "four sets of laws and four sets of agencies, who in the hell is in charge?" It was only logical to see and predict more legal action in the future.

CHAPTER 16

SURPREME COURT AND MODERNIZATION PLAN

PERMIT TO DUMP WATER INTO CREEK AND PACIFIC

Casmalia Resources had always been required to keep all liquids including rainwater from leaving the site by the local state Water Board, but on Oct. 17'[1] they applied for a permit to dispose of millions of gallons of marginally hazardous water into the creek south of the hazardous site which then runs in back of the Casmalia School District's playground. If granted it would be a big change for the facility and for our community. This is the same operator that illegally dumped water into the creek years ago without a permit. It was estimated that the amount of marginally hazardous water would have been between 66 million and 125 million gallons. Casmalia Resources needed to get rid of the liquids to comply with the state Toxic Pits Cleanup Act. Transport of the liquids to Kettleman Hills toxic dump site would cost an estimated $152 million and would require 140 to 170 truckloads per day for 10 months. The staff at the local Regional Water Board first had to review the application and the information submitted. Casmalia Resources was also applying for a permit to be exempted from the Toxic Pit Cleanup Act. The staff was also reviewing this request. Hunter as part of his scam was checking out every available angle to keep that money flowing!

On Nov. 4th the local state Water Board finally did what Dr. Hart and the County had immediately done and set a deadline for additional testing on offsite contamination migration.

The deadline was set for Nov. 30th, but the officials still glossed over the fact that there was already evidence of offsite migration of contaminates in the first round of tests. The real issue was how far had it migrated beyond the first offsite testing?

MORE JURISDICTIONAL QUESTIONS

With the last jurisdictional lawsuit about county authority still being appealed to the State Supreme Court, another jurisdictional dispute between the county and state over Casmalia Resources toxic dumpsite was brewing as the firm was seeking to implement the "Modernization Plan". County staff, led by Larry Appel, the North County Resource Management Chief, was to ask the Board of Supervisors to fight for shared or primary authority over the new plan. Larry made his home in Orcutt and was attuned to North County problems. The firm wanted permission to discharge treated wastes into Casmalia Creek, close and clean up existing ponds and construct new treatment facilities, lined ponds, reopen its PCB landfill, and construct a new on-site office complex.

Apple explained to the board of supervisors, "We believe a conditional use permit is necessary (for grading, building and discharge), but Casmalia says it doesn't need the permit. We are not going to issue permits until they're in compliance with a new Conditional Use Permit. Casmalia Resources has applied for the modernization plan' with the state Department of Health Services and claims the county has no jurisdiction. Despite the states' primary authority that shouldn't preclude local permits. An environmental impact report is needed in any case, but the state has refused to share lead agency status with the county and I want you to challenge the state's decision. Notice was received on Oct. 26th and we have until Nov. 26 to challenge the process." No decision was made on this request from Larry Appel on this issue at the supervisor's meeting.

Later, after the supervisor's green light, Dianne Guzman, the county's Resource Management Department Director, filed an appeal with the state Office of Planning and Research requesting lead agency status. In the appeal she said, " It is a governmental entity of more general jurisdiction than the state DHS and has vastly more experience than the state in preparing EIRs. Santa Barbara County should have jurisdiction because of the county zoning ordinance requires a land use permit before using any structure, or commencing any work pertaining to the erection, moving, alteration, enlarging, or rebuilding of any building, structure, or improvement within the county."

But Gov. George Deukmejian stepped into the decision process of the county request and ruled that the state Department of Health Services is the primary agency to oversee an environmental study for a major improvement program at Casmalia Resources. This was a setback for the County of Santa Barbara. While the finding carries no legal weight the attorney for Casmalia Resources said, "The county has no discretionary land use decisions to make at this time because the modernization plan falls within the scope of the existing use permit and a 1986 agreement.

Dianne Guzman stated that, "Santa Barbara County had to appeal to the state health department as a first step before legal action could be filed. The state health department has a poor track record of preparation of environmental reports and a very poor record of sensitivity to environmental concepts. We think that the state is in the business of keeping Casmalia Resources open and they won't do an objective environmental review. We are very concerned that it will be a shoddy report."

Again, in Los Angeles Gov. George Deukmejian was making waves for his industrial contributors at a conference on solid waste management.

The Governor said in his presentation, " Unless we expand our landfill reserves, unless we increase our landfill capacity the amount of space for dumping waste will be gone by the year 2001." He asked for support in the state's efforts to build "effective processes to meet long-term waste management requirements." Since Casmalia Resources was the only site in the state proposing a new "modernization plan", he was talking about Casmalia Resources in his appeal to this group. Los Angeles may have needed, but far away and out of sight Casmalia and Santa Barbara County certainly did not need their waste.

The governor's speech was briefly delayed when two environment activists from Greenpeace yelled, "We won't let toxic waste burn and sicken our children." The Republican governor said, after the outburst and the protesters were removed from the room, "local officials must strive to stand above the crossfire between those who support and oppose locating new controversial sites for disposal facilities". Skeleton-costumed members of the Greenpeace staged a rally outside the hotel before the governor's speech. Bradly Angel, the San Francisco spokesman for Greenpeace said, "They see it all as a cure-all, a quick fix for the government and a big profit for industry, but they disregard the environment and public safety for us all."

ANGRY "MODERNIZATION PLAN" BUS PROTEST

Greenpeace and local residents from Casmalia next used a roadblock to air the Casmalia Community's message at the dump site's front gate. The entry was blocked for about an hour by using a school bus that was disabled and dragged across the road and abandoned after all the tires were deflated. Arrested for obstructing a roadway were Traci Rene Romine, 25, North Hollywood, William Harold Whiting, 40, San Francisco and Edward Luis Martinez III, 28, San Francisco. Romine was chained to the rear door of the bus. Whiting was chained inside and Martinez was chained to the driver's seat. Greg Trexler 36, from Los Angeles was also arrested for slashing the tires to prevent the sheriff's department from re-inflating them.

Bradly Angel, regional toxic campaign director for Greenpeace, said emphatically, "We were rather upset, as were a lot of local residents. We think we sent a clear message that people are just fed up with the dump. We are opposed to dump plans such as using unlined ponds beyond a state-mandated deadline and discharging treated waste from ponds into Casmalia Creek. The 37-foot bus, with slogans written on it such as, We Have a Dream of a Toxics Free Future; Caution, Children Breathing; Cap it, Close it, Clean it up. These slogans were effective and it was a particularly appropriate vehicle to use because of the dump's proximity to Casmalia's elementary school. It was the most poignant thing we could have done, to use the school bus." Greenpeace had sacrificed and had done wonders for the community. On Sunday 72 physicians in the Santa Maria Valley placed a signed advertisement in the Santa Barbara News Press calling for the immediate closure and cleanup of the toxic dump site. We owed both groups much for their efforts on our behalf.

Right after this event the community was out in force at a meeting put on at the Minami Center by the state Department of Health Services to explain the new "Modernization Plan". Nick Irmiter explained in his comments, "I thought a thorough cleaning is in order before any permits for new projects are allowed. If they're going to do a good clean up job, they have to go down until they don't find any more contaminated water or soil." Lew Dunn was even sharper in his criticism, "This is a death warrant for the people in the Santa Maria Valley and certainly in

Casmalia. No runoff, whether treated or not, should be allowed to leave the site, the original rules and regulations should be followed. Looking at their record it may not be safe after they've treated it." Jerry Corlew spoke up and said he agreed and added, "If you attempt it, we're going to put our bodies in it and if we get ill, it's on your heads. I do not put any faith in the track record of this company."

NEW APCD DIRECTOR RYERSON'S POLICY

On Thursday and Friday in early December 1987 I was forced to call in complaints about fumes and odors at the school to the county as 22 out of 29 students and staff reported respiratory problems as winds blew in from the direction of the toxic dump site. The APCD inspector responded to both the school and 14 other complaints in the community. It was great to have a quick and rapid response. James Ryerson the new director said an inspector from his staff identified odors in the town as the same as those at the dump. The odors seemed to come from Pond C that was being cleaned out. It was expected that this would only last another week. Unlike earlier responses the director ordered the site closed down for the weekend or until a change in wind directions and conditions. This was a far cry from how the community had been treated in the past and we greatly appreciated the new policy. In addition, the district's new engineering supervisor, Craig Strommen, said they were increasing the number of air samples being taken as a precaution. The community certainly appreciated the new growing positive relationship.

EPA REPORT AND STATE SUPREME COURT DECISION

The California State Supreme Court ruled at the end of 1987 that Santa Barbara County did have the right to exercise reasonable monitoring of the waste dump. The courts unanimously ruled in favor of the county. They held that state law did not bar "reasonable local regulation." As enacted, the ordinance did not prevent toxic waste disposal or treatment, but only requires Casmalia to comply with a monitoring program to determine whether the dump was a source of pollution. We do not find this unreasonable particularly in light of the state's findings at the 501 hearing. They further ruled, "There is no evidence to support the company's claim that compliance would cost as much as $9.4 million for the first year/' The county had won the right to regulate the dump.

At the beginning of 1988 a damming EPA report was released after the earlier visit and inspection by the EPA National Investigations Center from Denver that could result in significant fines by the agency. The report, congressional sources say, "is expected to be used as evidence for the need to close the Casmalia Plant." The report concluded Casmalia Resources failed to monitor the type of hazardous waste shipped to its treatment facility and did not keep adequate records in accordance with federal law. The report stated that, "an inspection of the records indicated that the site failed to obtain a detailed chemical and physical analyses of hazardous waste accepted for treatment or disposal. Examination of the facility files indicates that in most cases, no information was recorded for waste streams prior to arrival at the facility and no testing or insufficient testing was conducted when wastes were accepted for treatment or disposal. Also, guidelines for managing waste were violated in that they did not always follow the facility waste analysis plan. Records show they disposed or treated bulk waste without the information required by the plan. They were also unable to locate inspection reports for security systems, landfills, treatment facilities and surface impoundments. Waste ponds did not comply with regulations and provide for structural integrity. Slope failure and deep erosion channels were observed on nine ponds". My thought and comment was, "and to think the owner called this a state of the art facility and operation?" Rep. Bob Lagomarsino's comment was, "…the waste facility should be shut down and that the EPA had missed its own deadlines in the Casmalia Resources' inquiry.

The county won some and lost some challenges, but the important thing was that they were trying now to help the folks in Casmalia. Some events were good news and some were bad news. Many more challenges lay ahead, but we now had many helpers ranging from Greenpeace to some levels of government. I increasingly did not feel so alone in our quest and actually felt optimistic. Only time would tell!

CHAPTER 17

STATE CAPITOL PROTEST AND BUMPY CLEAN UP ROAD

COUNTY COURT CHALLEGE OF MODERNIZATION PLAN

Deputy County Counsel Jed Beebe wasted no time in exercising the county's State Supreme Court's affirmation of the right of " reasonable regulation" of the dump site. On the morning of March 7[1b] he asked the Santa Barbara County Superior Court to decide whether Casmalia Resources needed a new county permit to make proposed changes in the Modernization Plan. Casmalia Resources attorney Michael Cooney said, "…I am not surprised that the county filed suit, but we maintain that we do not need to file for new permits. It could take as long as six months until we submit our arguments." The longer they could drag it out the more cash flowed through the front gate. Beebe said, "The county Board of Supervisors would have to decide whether to allow Casmalia Resources to continue operations if the judge decided the dump needed new permits.

Beebe then gave a brief history of existing permits, "…they obtained the first permit in 1972 and the conditions have been updated several times since then. In 1986 the county entered into an agreement with Casmalia

Resources, which settled all existing questions regarding the consistency of the facility's operation with its existing permit. In that contract, the dump agreed to obtain land-use permits to build any additional facilities at the site. County zoning laws and the contract required permits for all the new proposals."

It was not until June 1988 that the local superior court decided that the dump site must obtain an amended county conditional use permit to build any additional facilities at the site. Casmalia lost this round as the judge ruled, "...the county has the right to participate in the permitting process.

DUMP OWNER'S RANT AND WIFE'S PRE-TRIAL HEARINGS

Jan Lachenmaier, the public relations director for the dump site, announced two new public relations events at the dump site on April 4th and again on April 15th to push the new Modernization Plan and put it in a much better public light. She said, "... we have received many questions about the pond-closure program and want to answer these." Director of engineering, Dan Ringstmeyer, headed the bus tour past half of the 42 ponds currently being cleaned. It was also on the day of the second event that Casmalia Resources announced a change of plans for the clean-up of the site.

They had received much criticism about plans to dump excess rainwater directly into Casmalia Creek. Instead, they will apply for a permit to use the water to irrigate the hillsides surrounding the site, according to Jim McBride, the general manager of the waste facility. The water, according to him, would be treated before being applied to the grassy slopes adjacent to the landfill. Thus, it was much the same as the way they used to spray toxic waste into the air to help speed up evaporation. They planned to submit plans in a few weeks to the local Regional Water Quality Board.

Mr. McBride said, "Their plan in October created quite a stir when they filed an application to dispose of millions of gallons of treated pond water into Casmalia Creek. Members of the Casmalia Community strongly opposed the plan and indicated site operators have a poor track record and should not be allowed to undertake any new projects. This is an attempt to come up with something more acceptable."

Hunter should have left the news conference and show to his subordinates, as his performance was testy, I am sure he was in a bad mood from all the ongoing pretrial hearings that his dear wife Nancy (the Golden Girl) Hunter was undergoing for her involvement in the J. David affair and swindle in San Diego. His subsequent rant revealed him to be the greedy noncaring person that he was.

During the question-and-answer session after the presentation he was asked about his old buddy DeWayne Holmdahl's suggestion and proposal that he should pay to relocate the residents of the nearby town of Casmalia. This set him off on a rant that was not good as far as public relations with the public in general. He first labeled it as only a "political gesture" with the election fast approaching. "We have 5,000 acres around the site. We are two miles away from the town "This is not true. This is only a short walk of $1^{1/2}$ miles to the school and the site sits on the edge of the 5,000 acres". It is a sufficient buffer. We certainly don't have the money to do something like that ourselves. Nothing has ever been shown to have left the site, we do have occasional odors, I'm sure, but everything can't be blamed on the toxic dump site." This picture was painted by a man who lived in wealthy Montecito and owned three large golf courses on the California Central Coast.

He was then asked about the $1 billion lawsuit. He railed, "I will not agree to an out of court settlement. I don't want to settle. I think we have a solid case and we want to prove it." He also added and told reporters," I do not see a need to get a new conditional use permit from the county. We have had a permit for 16 or 17 years." The county of course disagreed and sued for new permits before the site could go ahead with the big reconstruction plans in the works. The stress in Hunter's voice was obvious to the reporters present that day. It was understandable because he had many personal and business issues to deal with and I am sure he was beginning to feel the pressure, but with any good scheme he had plenty of money to hire lawyers and give everyone from San Diego to Santa Barbara County a run tor their money!

ELECTION TIME

As election time neared in Lompoc for DeWayne Holmdahl's seat, which was the town in the center of DeWayne Holmdahl's district, a reporter from the local Lompoc Record by the name of Samuel Cope decided to do a story about how Casmalia residents rated politicians on assisting them with dump woes. He used me as the contact for the community of Casmalia and doctors Leo Armstrong and Dan DuCoffe from the Physicians Against Casmalia Resources as other opponent contacts.

INSURANCE INVESTIGATOR AND EPA FINE

When I saw the news story about the EPA fine levied against the dump site for lack of liability insurance and the lack of deposits in the closure trust fund account, my mind flashed back to around the first of the year and the young professional Insurance Investigator who came into my office after school one day. I now realized that at the time that I had made the right I decision about not talking or on the other hand talking with the investigator. It set me back when he gave me his card and introduced himself as working for Kenneth Hunter's insurance carriers. I knew from law school that these companies would be the ones stuck with the costs of any major part of any recovery, so it made me leery of talking with him at first. They had a vested interest in protecting the insured and themselves, but it did seem that his mission was to get at the facts for some sort of company decision.

But we hit it off well and I asked him to sit down and I settled down in my chair behind the principal's desk. It dawned on me as we exchanged pleasantries that anything, I had to say had been said by me many times in the media and that nothing I would say would be new to our community's opponents at the dump site. So, when we got to specifics, I let Casmalia's story unfold. I started from the very beginning and told of every violation, event and occurrence as I moved forward in time with the story. We talked for about two hours in my office and I was late getting home from work on this day. It dawned on me as I was reading about the large EPA fine, that he had been evaluating the continuation of the site's liability insurance.

Apparently, I had helped them to decide to cancel the policies and so it was a worthwhile visit with a sympathetic investigator

The fines were based on the company's failure to deposit money m accounts to eventually close the site and to show proof of adequate liability insurance. The fine was set at $313,000 for the failures. They had 30 days to submit proof of having made the $7.8 million deposit into the trust fund and 60 days to present documentation of liability insurance totaling $8 million. Lochenmaler said, "The company recently bought a $5.2 million certificate of deposit from the state". She said she doubted that any, "facility in the nation is able to get conventional insurance." I didn't know about other sites but I thought to myself this site with all its shenanigans can't get the liability insurance! She went on to say, "We feel we have adequate funds in the closure trust account because most of the surface ponds have been closed." It made me feel warm, good, and satisfied to know I had helped to create more headaches for Kenneth Hunter and his efforts to keep the scam going. How much longer would the scam last?

STATE CAPITOL PROTEST

The state capitol protest was the most ambitious of all our efforts and it was carefully planned by Kathie Hoxie, and other local environmentalists working with Bradly Angel, from Greenpeace, in San Francisco, We were transporting a group of 75, a third of the population, to Sacramento to confront the governor and the state health director. We would be asking for help and asking for the resignation of the health director. The lofty goal of the resignation I am sure, would not occur, but the whole trip would generate much state wide publicity. Greenpeace secured a large bus to transport the community including school children to this event. It was a long trip and required an early departure. We planned a rally on the capitol steps, a march to the governor's office inside the capitol building, and then on to the health director's office located in another building.

Prior to the departure date I started to fool around with an old coloring book with pigs on the front. It reminded me of Dr. Kizer so I started thinking what a great tool for our planned mock classroom on the capitol steps. I did the front page and then Meg, the secretary, and others took it from there. It became a derogatory training coloring book for state health workers. It was quite humorous and Meg loved it. It was right down her alley humor wise. Copies were made and It was quite a hit and was passed out at all three locations on the day of the event.

It was summer time and perfect weather for the trip. A few days prior to the trip I had a family emergency that almost resulted in me not going, but Greenpeace pitched in for airline tickets for me and my young son to fly to Sacramento. It was my son's first airline flight and that turned out to be quite an event because as we neared the Sacramento Airport, we started to hit severe wind turbulence that dropped the plane many feet each time we hit one. Finally, after landing we were picked up at the airport by Kathie Hoxie and her sister for the ride to the capitol steps. Kathie's sister was into the local scuttle-butt of Sacramento and told us about one of our local representatives from the central coast not planning to run. It was advanced notice that would give some opponent an advantage to get ready for a run. At the time it meant nothing to me, but Kathie and her sister were very intent and interested in the discussion of this subject. I just figured being in the environmental movement they were naturally also into politics.

As planned, we set up the mock classroom were parents and children told reporters the dump was responsible for deaths and illness in their town. In my short presentation I stated, "…between 50% and 90% of the students at the school suffer from respiratory illness. The school and town are 1 ½ miles from the toxic waste dump." An emotional Ramona Ramirez said, "…my kids are always sick. Please help us and close it down." Jerry Corlew said, "We refuse to be sacrificed so that industry has a convenient place to dump its poisons." It was further explained that despite repeated appeals by residents to shut down the toxic dump site, the state allows the facility to continue operating. Briefly, the Lt. Governor said a few words of support and then it was off to the governor's office. On the way we all chanted, "Hey governor, don't you know, toxic waste has got to go." Naturally, he was not in, but we did get some good news photos in his office that appeared state wide and locally in the Santa Barbara Newspress.

In addition to our coloring book, we left a copy of a letter for the governor which read in part, "…it is obvious that Dr. Kizer is insensitive to our situation. It is clear that his intentions are to keep the dump open and operating, despite any and all evidence of the damage it is causing to our families and those of surrounding communities."

Classified

Santa Barbara News Press

**Residents, teachers and students from Casmalia
marched Into the governor's office In Sacramento**

CHAPTER 18

EVENING RENDEZUOUS AND ONE MORE COFFIN NAIL

MANY HEARINGS FOR SITE CLEAN UP

Because of my school responsibilities I was unable to attend many upcoming hearings and meetings scheduled, but Jerry and Nick were present in force representing our interests. The first of these was a hearing by the water board to consider an extension request of the clean-up that was state mandated.

While the Regional Water Quality Control Board treated Casmalia Resources with kid gloves and a sizable dose of leniency not everyone at the hearing was so fortunate. The City of San Luis Obispo received a $125,000 fine and a referral to the district attorney for an investigation of possible criminal conduct in the city's handling of waste discharges. It appeared that the city administrator and city council were aware of the problem.

The biggest winner at the hearing was Casmalia Resources who achieved its goal of an extension of the clean up deadline. Nick Irmiter testified, " There's already a time schedule, June 30, 1988—Let's get with it, please." Attorney Marc Chytilo representing Physicians Against Casmalia argued, "Casmalia's continued receipt of liquid waste for neutralization slow processing the toxic liquid remaining in the nine ponds by tying up equipment and resources." Leonard, the director, was considering requiring the company to show that accepting additional wastes would not affect the cleanup process. The Santa Barbara County Board of Supervisors and Assemblyman Jack O'Connell urges fines be levied and the cleanup be pushed forward. In response to all the testimony no fine was levied and the cease-and-desist order was unanimously approved with a new clean up deadline set for November 1,1988. Now there were rumors that the EPA, as a result of it, investigation by the Denver Team, might deny Casmalia a permit. "If the permit is denied we will appeal the order" according to Jan Lachenmaier, the public relations director for the dump site. She then said, "The dump will continue to operate until the final decision is made." Hunter seemed to have unlimited funds to hire lawyers to appeal and appeal. Nothing seemed to stop the flow of money into this site.

To add insult to injury the next step for the dump site was to excavate pond 19 which was filled with hydrofluoric acid which is one of the more reactive of the acids. This was part of the sites cleanup plan. Casmalia residents were up in arms when the local hospitals were notified to be prepared in case of possible exposures caused by spills or leaks, but no notification was given to residents of Casmalia. It was another example of do the work first and then get permits and on this occasion, to fail to notify nearby residents and take other needed precautions. Nick Irmiter angrily said at our press conference at the school, "We feel we should have been notified if they're going to be doing work like this." Lachenmaier responded later for the dump that, "This work is just one more step in the pond closures and modification plan and we didn't view it as out of the ordinary." Strange that they saw it necessary to notified the hospitals about their own workers, but not us!

It was my turn to speak and I tried to pounce on them saying that, "The possibility that hydrofluoric acid, which is extremely deadly, could be blown toward the community and school raised the question, again, of why there is no evacuation plan for this school district and community? In November of 1985 I pointed out to the County of Santa Barbara that our exit to the west is blocked by the air force base and if the east road is blocked, we are trapped." Bruce Lee for the county said, "The answer was simple: I've never been told there was a hazard. The site was checked for flammability and the risks were insignificant, there was nothing to justify creating an evacuation plan. If there had been a flammability risk, I would have developed a plan." I guess the county had not thought of checking for all other types of risk such as windblown fumes into lower adjacent valleys. I thought his explanation was shocking when I read it in the news story and this made me even angrier! It showed the callus safety disregard that the county had shown toward the community in past years.

Shortly after the news report I, with the help of Meg, prepared a second request for an. evacuation plan for the community and school district. On August 26th, shortly after the bad publicity, they finally concurred that we needed one and started working on it. It's amazing how a lawsuit and other public efforts can change their point of view.

By Aug. 29th I received a letter back and a copy of the plan. I responded in another short news conference in front of the school with, "We really respect Lee for the speed with which he acted in this matter. The first target of the plan would be the orderly operation at pond 19 because of its dangerous contents. The contents will kill you if you breathe a small amount. Environmental Health services will be stationing trained personnel equipped with portable radios so that proper authorities can be notified immediately in case of accident. In case of accident the fire department Hazardous Material Team will respond, the Air Pollution Control District, Sheriff's Department, California Highway Patrol, and additional Environmental Health Service staff would immediately be dispatched to the scene. The Air Pollution Control District has tied its computer into the weather station at Casmalia to help assess the threat from a reported accident more accurately. If evacuation is ever imminent residents would be informed by methods such as loudspeaker and door-to-door notification."

Another hearing was planned on Aug. 14th at the Veterans Memorial Center in Santa Maria to deal with site violations that could at least help to close Casmalia Resources. At a brief news conference on the school's front lawn I stated, "Opponents of the site are already planning to be present in force at the hearing. We are gearing up for it. We are hoping to coordinate a large turnout of Santa Maria residents." Kathie Hoxie told the news media, "The press conference will be held outside the Veterans Hall just before the hearing at about 6:30 PM. We are going to talk about what we hope the EPA will do. We're hoping Congressman Lagomarsino will be able to come down and speak." On the day of the hearing the permit was on the line or a serious fine or both, but only time and events would tell.

The hearing was for the purpose of discussing the EPA's tentative decision to deny a Recourse Conservation and Recovery Act permit and did not accomplish much. Jan Lachenmeier speaking for the dump site said, "Even if they deny our permit we will go ahead with planned construction. We can appeal it to Washington, and during that appeals process, we can continue to operate our four existing landfills under the conditions of our interim status permit. And then, during that time, we can build our modernization plant and create new lined landfills. The appeals process could take anywhere from a few months to a year. We feel confident that the EPA will in fact grant the permit. They have expressed to us that their tentative denial was based on a lack of information, so we are currently giving them additional data and will continue to do so until they make their decision."

Strangely enough, Nick Irmiter agreed saying, " I will grant the permit because they don't know what else to do. Of course, they are for it. They're just going to say the b.s. they've been saying all along. You don't need a year for that. But they have to be aware that we're going to go tooth and nail all the way, and keep on fighting until eventually they are closed. If they want to keep going for years and years, there's not much we can do about their decision, but they're just making money off our health."

Eventually the EPA announced that it was going to grant the dump site a hearing on which the date was to be set at a later time. The EPA was to have made its final decision by Nov 8th, but the decision for the hearing was net announced until Nov. 15th. Nick was understandably upset at all the delays and said to me, "This could go on for years and years and while waiting they continue to operate."

ABOUT FACE ON COUNTY PERMITS

Just as with the $200 million Jerry Dominelli scheme of love, power and greed in San Diego in Southern California this scam also showed the power of money and being able to manipulate regulators and the system with attorneys. Now Hunter was changing course after bogging down the county in court for months on end.

County Supervisor Toru Miyoshi announced the supposed good news. Casmalia Resources, who had already held the county back for six months, announced an agreement with the operators of Casmalia Resources. They had agreed to apply for new county permits before going ahead with plans to construct the new facilities. He said, " We find this a major change in attitude of the facility owners and a clear victory for Santa Barbara County."

The announcement followed by one day a vote of 3-2 by the county supervisors to require an amended land use permit rather than a piecemeal expansion of the site. The community of Casmalia's long-time nemesis, DeWayne Holmdahl, voted against the proposal and it was said at the meeting, "…any applicant other than Casmalia would have been allowed the minor expansion. I suggest the firm has been discriminated against because of the dump's unpopularity." He should have been thinking more about his own unpopularity.

Miyoshi went on to say, "… the county could attach several conditions to the permit including a requirement to clean up contaminated ground water and to extend the buffer zone. If the buffer zone was expanded

Casmalia Resources probably would have to buy up property 1^{1}/z miles away in the town of Casmalia; the property that residents say they have been unable to sell."

MY EVENING RENDEZUOUS

It had been a quite normal day at school and in the afternoon, after everyone left, I set in the principal's office working on state school reports when the phone rang. A voice on the end of the line said in a raspy tone, "Is this Mr. McCalip the school principal?" "Yes, can I help you?" I responded. He said, " I am a night time employee at Casmalia Resources and I have some information I want to give you. It is important and I think it will be extremely important to your efforts." This piqued my interest and I responded that, "It would be great. Can you bring it over to the school?" He responded, " No, I would prefer you meet me tonight out at the corner of NTU road, just park your car at the corner and walk about half way up and I will meet you half way. Let's say about 9:00 this evening? I don't want anyone to know about this contact." In response I answered, "That sounds good. I will see you at 9:00 this evening."

Being the worry wart that I am, I immediately started to ponder whether this was a safe and prudent move. My mind flashed back to being driven off the road by the disgruntled employee right after I started appearing on TV frequently. Was this just another disgruntled employee interested in doing me some harm? I thought maybe I should take a gun just to be safe, but I don't even own one. So, to say the least, I was apprehensive. That evening I am sure I did some nervous pacing, but tried to keep it under control so the family wouldn't notice. At 8:30 I told my wife, Pernelle, that I needed to run to the hardware store for some items I needed for the weekend.

When I arrived at the designated location at the corner of NTU road leading to the dump site I parked my car off the main highway and got out and started up the darkened road leading to the dump entrance.

The moon was obscured out by coastal fog and was not full. When I had gone about ½ miles, I saw a shadowy figure moving toward me from the direction of the dump site entrance and the office complex. We met about half way and to my relief he was caring survey rolls and a large packet of documents and not a weapon. I recognized the raspy voice from the phone call. We talked only briefly, but before we went our separate ways, I asked what the documents would show. In his now-familiar voice he replied, "Massive illegal overfilling beyond permit requirements. Do what you think best with them." I thanked him and thanked him again on behalf of the entire community. Boy! was I relieved to get out of their safely. This sounded like and event changer if it proved to be true.

Later, when I had time to take a good look at the information, I found it was data and copies of the survey work done by Hunter's own engineers. The next day after having copies made, Meg and I worked on getting a certified return receipt package ready, with a brief letter from me, to mail off to the EPA office in far off San Francisco.

The EPA wasted no time in announcing it was fining the site $6.2 million for landfilling 260,000 cubic yards of hazardous waste more than its current permit allows. Casmalia's total authorized capacity is 2.6 million cubic yards. The dump was given 30 days to respond to the allegations or pay the fine. The same announcement also notified the public that they were releasing the proposed new permits for the dump site for public review with more hearings to be scheduled at a later date. At the time, nationally, it was the largest fine ever issued by the EPA. I started to get that warm fuzzy feeling when I first read the news and was happy again that I had helped to create another headache for the operators of the facility. I, naturally, will be forever grateful to the dump employee who provided the information.

CHAPTER 19

LOCAL JUDGE IN THE COURT OF PUBLIC OPINION

THE LEGAL ANGLE

Up until this time Hunter's organization appeared to be a stone wall of resistance as exemplified by his rant at the dump tour a few years ago about never settling out of court. He had money and power to manipulate regulators, judges, and politicians at all levels of government. It was this scam's stone wall that needed to start to crumble before we would have any type of justice for the folks trapped in the small town of Casmalia. My determination and optimism was now running high. We had many successes, the $6.2 million fine we helped to arrange by mailing the technical information to the EPA, the slow conversion of the County of Santa Barbara into a reluctant ally after out disclosure of the damming Air Pollution Control documents discovered in the public files and the law suit later filed against the county, the cancellation of the toxic dump's liability insurance helped along by discussions with the insurance investigator for Hunter's Insurance companies. All of these had chipped away at his stone wall. I was geared up and buoyed for further success and hoped it would come the community's way, but other local roadblocks now developed.

146

We were now represented by three law firms; Richard Brenneman from Santa Maria; Toxie Hall Smith from the Los Angeles area; and Robert Sulnick the law professor from Loyola University in the Los Angeles area. A new lawyer from Alaska, William Van Doren who worked for all the law firms on our team, opened a rented office in Santa Maria specifically to handle the Casmalia case. Bill and I became good friends in the course of events. His branch office was located in office space along the main street of Santa Maria. The local office was set up for the now over 332 clients that needed work ups of basic information and for a deposition location as well as for deposition preparation. It was a massive undertaking with this many clients. I was pleased when the law firms asked to use my video as a preparation of plaintiffs for depositions. It was a good summation of the community's experiences

Although I was never called for a deposition my wife was. She had to travel to Santa Barbara for the event. My wife is tall and good looking and knows how to take care of herself in the public arena. The attorney for Hunter at the law firm was short and squatty and was intimidated by her appearance and demeanor. I am sure he expected a poor person dressed poorly, having difficulty articulating responses, but this she was not. Pernelle and I had lost a child, a girl, with a still birth before my son John and later Meghan were born. This was the main focus of his interrogation that full day in Santa Barbara. After a full morning of questions about our health prior to the still birth, after lunch he started again with the same questions only differently worded. My wife asked for some of the stenographer paper and proceeeded to fold paper to make origami birds and animals as she sat there pausing before answering each question. Little did he know she had just finished to is as an art lesson with her students at school. Her appearance coupled with the origami exercise rattled his cage. He was probably happy to let her go early that day.

Legal wrangling continued in the local Superior Court in front of Judge Zel Canter. The most recent hearing was a request for more information on medical records to be provided by our attorneys. Robert Sulnick argued, "I have provided all the documents both sides previously agreed to share, which was 15 percent sample of the medical records." Judge Canter granted the request for the dump site and ordered our attorney to turn over the medical records. The Judge also warned our attorneys of the five-year statute of limitations which runs out in two years on the original suit.

Within three days of this hearing Casmalia Resources was faced with a new suit. The new suit made some of the same allegations and lists the same defendants and plaintiffs as the one filed in 1985 as well as asking for about $1 billion in damages. Attorney Brenneman commented that, "It was done to preserve the rights of the plaintiffs to make claims for damages since the first suit was filed. If we didn't file this, they would claim we could not claim damages that have occurred from continuing exposure and further damages. It also alleges that Casmalia Resources failed to comply with the mandates of Proposition 65, which requires businesses to notify the public about releases of toxic chemicals. Under the provision of that 1986 initiative, private citizen may seek damages up to $2,500 per day per exposure if state and federal authorities fail to act on reported violations."

One of our law firms contacted me to let me know, before Bill Van Doren set up the Santa Maria Office, that another new law firm was joining the effort. It was information that I am sure would get Hunter's attention. When you are running a scam like the dump using lawyers at every turn it is important that you have more funds to work with than your opponent. This is why I was extremely pleased to learn that the Herbert Hafif law firm was joining the team. He was fresh from the BKK waste facility suit which involved 508 plaintiffs and which received a collective settlement of $45 million in 1986 after four years in court. He had the legal clout and funds to carry the community's suit to a successful conclusion. My comment to the press when they called after the announcement in Los Angeles was that, "The entire community is pleased with Hafif's involvement and we are sure the suit will now move along quickly." I am sure this announcement got Hunter's attention as he was now having serious concurrent legal problems in San Diego with his new wife's trial where a former accountant was giving damaging testimony concerning her involvement in the J. David scam. Our new financially powerful law firm flipped the rules of the game for Hunter and increased his woes!

It was at this time that Hunter decided to give one of his now infamous dump press conferences. What he said that day was revealing in that it showed he was beginning to feel the heat and was again lashing out. Hunter joined other Casmalia Resources officials at the news conference to acquaint reporters with recent changes at the site. If he had been smart, he would have stayed home and let his staff handle the event. He used it to announce, " That because of licensing hurdles and changing state regulations that the site may have to temporarily shut down at the end of the year, during a period of site reconstruction". Hunter also used the opportunity to chide the press for focusing on what he referred to as, "the bizarre and eye-catching and he took politicians to task for savaging the site." The state Regional Water Board had recently levied a $130,000 fine for both on and off-site water contamination.

Hunter said, apparently expecting sympathy that, "It's just not fair. We don't deserve that fine, but it takes $130,000 to fight it."

Next, in the performance to demonstrate his confidence in the safety of the site, he took a small sip of some ground water that had been pumped from one of the new wells. Jim McBride, the general manager, also took a sip saying, "I wouldn't be afraid to bathe my kids in this. During the lengthy permitting and construction phase, the site had hoped to keep its four existing landfills open. However, because unlined landfills are no longer allowed since they don't meet the standards, this will cause the shut down." So, the underlying theme of the dog and pony show told me that he was now concerned about expenses and money with all the pending fines and law suits coming his way. It was good news for us!

COMMUNITY'S MAJOR LEGAL OBSTACLE EMERGES

I often wondered whether our next protagonist, who was in the legal system, was mentally impaired and stupid or just extremely arrogant or possibly suffered from a little of both. His decisions were frequently illogical and showed a great lack of understanding of the Code of Ethics of the legal profession and Cannons of Conduct expected of Judges. His actions and court statements were extremely offensive to the community and his poor judgment was particularly offensive to me after clerking for a Superior Court Judge in Los Angeles of the highest integrity. He just did not measure up and his shenanigans made my blood boil. I was outraged by his comments and actions. As the situation developed, he would understand my right to exercise my freedom of speech as well as my anger. Unlike attorneys in his court room, he would have zero control over my opinions, actions, and statements. He would also be dealing with a group of individuals who, by 1990, were no longer novices in the field of public relations and their relationship with the news media.

At the end of 1989, our attorney, Robert Sulnick, argued against a change of venue request made by the dump site in the court room of Judge Royce Lewellen in Santa Maria. The dump owner's attorney argued that his client could not receive a fair trial in Santa Maria because of the amount of negative publicity that has been generated. The plaintiffs he said, "have been out there generating this publicity with mock funerals and have even hanged my client in effigy." He also showed a telephone poll conducted by the firm that showed only 20 percent of Kern County residents had heard of the dump site vs. close to 80 percent in Santa Barbara County who had a negative impression of the site. He failed to mention that Ventura County had a very similar percentage to Kern County and was a much more logical location on a well-traveled roadway with public transportation.

Robert Sulnick pointed out that, "It isn't fair to expect my clients, including one who is blind and another with terminal cancer to travel long distances on the dangerous and winding route 166. It would be more reasonable to relocate the trial to Ventura County, because there is public transportation between Santa Maria and Ventura. There is no bus transportation between Santa Maria and Bakersfield, the Kern County seat, and we are talking about the poor and infirmed." Lewellen brushed this off and said with no sensitivity that route 166 was not so bad that he had even gone hunting along the road. He said, "there is a far greater chance for a fair trial in Kern County, and Kern County is able to deal with civil cases faster that Ventura County. If this isn't a case for a change of venue, one never existed." He ordered the case moved to Kern County. He then added, "It is inconvenient, no question about it, but it is inconceivable that the trial could be held in Santa Barbara County with any pretense of fairness." Robert responded to the ruling saying he would be appealing the decision.

Meanwhile, Kern County turned down the offer of the Casmalia lawsuit because of an existing backlog. Lewellen said a new location may be needed to be found and also said he may have to disqualify himself because plaintiff's attorneys had filed a motion to have him taken off the case for alleged bias.

After the absurd ruling in the change of venue hearing, I could see blood, and being about to explode with anger, wrote the following letter to the editor which summed up my feelings:

"The Casmalia dump situation through the years has brought out both the best and worst in individuals in all endeavors ranging from health officials to politicians and more recently members of the bench.

Casmalia's story is a tragic example of the failure to shift regulatory control from the federal level to local officials who lack the expertise and political clout to handle this task. It is also the story of placing the burden of toxic waste disposal on the backs of poor people, the least capable of coping with these problems. Deregulation has been used by the dump operator to his advantage at every opportunity.

Most judges in the Santa Maria Valley have acted responsibly; they should be commended. Judge Royce R. Lewellen has established a track record that does not place him within the zone of decisions that a reasonable person would make or should make.

In the course of ruling on issues in this change of venue case he has made the following absurd decisions: First, he imposed sanctions on the community of Casmalia for delay when in fact the first delay was caused by the judge not being prepared. The second delay was caused by opposing counsel not following proper court procedures. The third delay was again caused by the court not being prepared. At no time were any of these delays caused by attorneys for the community of Casmalia, yet Judge Lewellen imposed a $300 sanction.

In a related matter, he ruled on a change-of-venue motion against the community of Casmalia and, based on statements made at the hearing, he very clearly had preconceived notions concerning the matter he was hearing. He ordered the trial moved to the most inconvenient location, Bakersfield, despite the fact that many of the townsfolks are injured, infirmed, old and sick. He refused to listen to case law that required the court to consider these factors.

Finally, when it was pointed out that many of the old and sick townfolks are depended on public transportation and none exist on Highway 166 to Bakersfield, he responded, "I am a backpacker and like to go both ways across 166... it's a beautiful road to travel certain times of the year." His response was hardly rational and certainly does not show an understanding of the needs of poor people.

Because of apparent conflict of interest, Judge Lewellen should voluntarily disqualify himself from hearing this case. If not, maybe it's time that voters permanently disqualify him so that we have a new judge making reasonable decisions. Not only is the dump owner entitled to a fair and impartial trial, so are the poor folks in Casmalia."

An out-of-town judge was brought in to hear the disqualification motion against Lewellen. In the meantime, private investigators for the community dug into the judge's past and found that he owned about a 20% interest in a family trucking firm in Missouri where he grew up. The investigator was also able to get a bid from the company to haul a load of toxic waste. So he had a direct financial interest in the industry he was making decisions about. In addition, the investigators found that he belonged to the same social clubs as the dump site owners and also played golf with them on occasion at the local golf course. I was optimistic about the upcoming ruling as it seemed like a slam dunk.

When Robert Sulnick called with the bad news that the visiting judge had ruled that he was not biased and not disqualified, our conversation was short other than Robert saying that this would be quite an obstacle having to transport the town folks and would make it harder to reach a settlement because the opposition would know of our pending difficulties.

I used to tease my own children about the fact that I was part Cherokee Indian and if they made me mad that my feathers would automatically grow out my head. When they were very young their wide eyes would search my head for any sign of where the feathers would emerge. Boy! If I was mad earlier when I wrote the letter to the editor, I must have had a full Indian head dress on because I was outraged!

Immediately after getting off the phone with the attorney I began calling all my allies and contacts to let them know I was heading down to the court house to put this bastard on trial "in the court of public opinion". We needed an immediate picket event! Next, I called all the media outlets on my list and then I was off to the court house with my mega phone and hoping that it would be more than me at the court house.

We ended up with about ten or twelve protesters with signs. We set up our picket line in the court house parking lot. I quickly explained the Cannons of Judicial Ethics to them and that judges are forbidden to hear cases in which "a mere appearance of impropriety appears". If that occurs, they are supposed to automatically disqualify themselves. So, I emphasized again to everyone, just in case they were interviewed, that the rule and key words were "mere appearance!" The community of Casmalia does not want this judge anywhere near our case.

When the TV news media started to arrive, I quickly went into my now-familiar one-on-one mode of interview. I started off by explaining the code of ethics about "a mere appearance" was the standard and that I wanted the news reporters to ask the judge to disqualify himself in front of the cameras. Please tell him that the entire community does not want him on this case because of the judicial standard he is not following. I then gave them details of the trucking firm and the social contacts and then reminded them of the standard "mere appearance". Today we were putting him on trial in the "court of public opinion". Kathie Hoxie also gave some interviews and then off the TV crews went into the court house to talk to the judge and put him on the spot. Soon the crews and reporters all returned with big smiles on their faces. He had disqualified himself in front of the cameras and the effort had paid off. I again had that warm fuzzy feeling of success. The next day several of the newspapers who were there called both Kathie, the judge, and I to get more detail for their stories. The judge skimmed over the fact of the judicial standard and said he was not biased and Kathie and I hit on it hard. It was the "mere appearance" that was at issue.

It was sometime later that I received a call from Attorney Bill Van Doren, who worked for us in the Santa Maria Office, that Robert Sulnick needed my help concerning my public trial of Judge Lewellen. Lewellen had the audacity to file charges against Robert with the State Bar Association contending that he had put me up to the protest at the court house that day. It could not have been further from the truth as Sulnick had nothing whatsoever to do with my actions. My actions had been dictated by my extreme anger and frustration. I knew on my own my freedom of speech rights. I did not need Robert and he did not even know about it I am sure until it was over as he was probably driving back to his home in Los Angeles.

Bill and I prepared a sworn written declaration for Robert to present at his hearing that stated that I was exercising my right to free speech and Robert knew nothing of my actions. It was totally my idea and that I was offended and angry by the judge's failure to properly follow the Code of Judicial Conduct and disqualify him when a mere appearance of impropriety existed.

I continued to view Judge Lewellen as either stupid or arrogant or more than likely both. He would not let the matter drop, which would have been wise of him, and he and others continued to write response letters to my earlier letter to the editors of local papers. So tit for tat letters kept the story alive until we got closer to an election cycle and I could not believe what Lewellen did next. They must not have good law schools in his home state of Missouri.

Lewellen did rule on another case between Casmalia Resources and the County of Santa Barbara and was equally absurd in his illogical thinking. Casmalia was going to use a hardening agent to clean up existing toxic liquids ponds and they decided they needed more liquid toxic waste to mix with what they already had. What a great plan to keep funds rolling through the front gate during cleanup. Could they convince a judge of its merits after the county cracked down on the proposed scheme by bringing an action to stop it? Sure, they could with good old Judge Lewellen who obliged his social buddies and his industry by saying yes you needed more waste to mix with the waste you already were trying to get rid of. I responded to the media saying "My reasoning is impaired and faulty." I thought to myself is this judge functioning with a full deck and thank god at least we had got him off the community's case. Luckly, Jed Beebe, the county counsel, pointed out that despite today's ruling, before they could import any additional waste, they had to first secure a land-use permit and we had made it clear that we will issue a permit "only for a non-hazardous alternative."

I had been so out front on the last confrontations that I let Nick Irmiter take this next one. Judge Lewellen next endorsed a challenger for Fifth District

Supervisor, a man named Attorney Mike Stoker, who had move to Santa Maria for the expressed purpose of running for office. This endorsement move was clearly against the code of judicial conduct. It was the most stupid and arrogant maneuver that I had ever witnessed and personally offended me after working as the clerk for Los Angeles Judge Paul Egley, who was a man of high personal integrity, when I was younger.

Nick laid it on thick, "Canon 7 states that Judges should not publicly endorse a candidate for non-judicial office and this includes retired judges upon recall to judicial service or prior to such service if they consider themselves available for such service and they shall comply with all provisions of this code." Irmiter went on to say, "the community will file charges against the judge with the California State Bar Association." Lewellen was unavailable for comment after this news event, so maybe, just maybe he was able to learn something! Later he disqualified.

CHAPTER 20

CRANSTON, CANCER DEATH, AND THE END GAME

FORUM AT THE VICTORIA STREET THEATER

The environmentalist in our group at the end of 1989 made arrangements for me to speak at a forum at the Victoria Street Theater in Santa Barbara with California Senator Alan Cranston. Cranston was reeling from a national Savings and Loan scandal. He was probably hoping that the Casmalia issue would be a distraction from his other woes. It was an excellent opportunity to get our message out, but I was apprehensive to say the least. It had been years since law school and my forced oral presentations in that process. To be quite frank, I never liked to do the oral presentations. This would be a large crowd and each person in the forum would be expected to make a presentation. Despite all my inner reservations, I agreed to go and I began my preparations as to what I would say. Normally, through these past few years I always spoke off the cuff and had no preparation. I just would begin talking and would wing it. This had been my method of operation for the TV media interviews and it proved to be for me a more relaxed and normal presentation. So, a few days prior to the event I pulled out a yellow legal pad and went to work on what I would say. My main purpose would be to get the EPA more involved in regulation and have them take over control of the dump site as the lead agency rather than the one that was the last resort. As usual I had lofty goals that were probably unattainable.

On the evening of the meeting, I arrived a little before starting time and was taken aback by the packed and overflowing theater. There was hardly room for the overflow standing crowd. It was even more terrifying than I had imagined in my wildest dreams. Luckily, they had name tags on the forum table set up on the stage and I noticed my spot was on the far right of the stage so I made my way to my location clutching my legal pad tightly in my hand. I noted I was seated next to a high-ranking EPA official. I thought to myself, derogatorily, where have you been all these years? I sat down in front of my mike and tried to get use to the large group. When the EPA official arrived, I made an extra effort to make small talk and establish rapport with him and tried to keep the conversation off our main subject for the evening.

In an instant it was my turn and I started my prepared presentation:

"Senator Cranston, thanks for being here in Santa Barbara County and thank you for having me on this forum. Today, I am here to give you the story of the small community of Casmalia and to ask you to go beyond commitment and for you to give us your pledge that you will seek an EPA investigation or, even better, a U.S. Senate Investigation of the toxic dump that has plagued our community. When this all began, I was taken aback by being called an environmental activist, but today I am proud to say I am an educator and an environmental activist.

Casmalia's tragic story is the failure to transfer toxic waste regulatory control to the local and state level from federal control -where it should be. State and local regulatory officials are all ill prepared to deal with industries and do not have the needed expertise and political clout needed.

And more importantly Casmalia's story is a tragic example of placing the burden of toxic waste disposal on the backs of poor people the least capable of dealing with this in our society.

Casmalia Resources has an exceeding bad record of violations through the years. Personally, I would not let this site owner baby sit my dog while I am on vacation or be allowed to expand the facility.

The violations include:

1972 flushing toxins down the creek in back of my school and a resulting reprimand.

1984 forcing me to close our school when children had no oxygen to breathe because it was replaced with cyanide gas and numerous other toxins.

1980-86 running the Zimpro Wet Air Oxidation Unit without permits

1980-86 spraying toxins into the air to enhance evaporation -resulting in $100,000 fine.

1986 the expansion of the site by 84 acres without permits.

1988 grading without permits and no testing for particulate matter.

1989 Exceeding permitted capacity with expected large EPA fine.

Despite all this evidence of intentional violations and at the very least Gross Negligence, the regulators are actually considering allowing this site to remain open and to expand.

Today we can sum up the federal response as too little too late. The federal government needs to be out front and not leading from the rear.

So today, Senator Cranston, I am asking you to join me as an environmental activist and to go beyond a mere comment to favor closure

—pledge to us that your will seek some type of federal investigation and action. Thank you."

I was taken aback by the rousing applause that followed my presentation as I was not anticipating any response. The next morning, I was given great reviews in the local papers for stealing the show. It took the message away from the Savings and Loan debacle that was also part of the panel discussion. As I made it for the door at the end of the forum, Kenneth Vaniter, whom I had not seen in the crowd from Casmalia, congratulated me for a job well done. Time would tell if this event had any impact!

ELDERLY CANCER DEATHS AND PROTESTERS

In August of 1990 Professor Jan Schienle of California State University at Northridge released more results of the health study which compared hair samples of 80 Casmalia residents with a control group in Arroyo Grande. It found that Casmalia Residents have twice as much arsenic, chromium and cadmium in their bodies as other Central Coast residents. Schienle said, "the findings are significant because all three metals evaluated are respiratory irritants, fibrotic agents causing emphysema and obstructive lung disease. The study is especially significant with respect to recent lung cancers among residents and are consistent with chromium exposures."

It stands to reason that the old and infirmed along with children were at greatest risk. It came as no shock to us all in Casmalia when it was announced that community icon Winifred Wollam, 81 had passed away at her son's home from lung cancer. She had it for quite a period and had lead a pure life with no smoking or drinking. In a 1984 interview with the Santa Barbara News- Press, she said she had no intention of leaving the community despite mounting concerns over the nearby hazardous waste facility. She said "I'd rather live right here and be happy." Prior to moving to Casmalia she lived in Los Olivos, Point Conception, and then Casmalia for 57 years. She was instrumental in developing the new school facility. She spent more than two decades on the school board, mostly as president. We were all saddened by her loss from lung cancer. I now had lost count of the lung related deaths!

At the next school board meeting I suggested that we change the school name to Winifred Wollam School, Casmalia School District in her honor. All agreed and we made arrangements for the event set for September 1st. At the name change event I said a few words about her service and added that what impressed me the most was that she "also tutored students at her home most of those years. I then turned the event over to County Superintendent Bill Cirone who lauded me for "the tenacity to hang in with the district during tough times." That was unexpected but was appreciated and made me feel wonderful.

But the person who really exhibited tenacity was 75-year-old Antonia Hernandez who had lived next door to the school during the entire time I worked for the school district. Since the passing of Mrs.Wollam she was the oldest resident of Casmalia. She always greeted me warmly when she was out in her back yard tending to her garden or other activities. Greenpeace had trained the community well and at this demonstration at the main gate resulted in many arrests. All eleven of those arrested were from Casmalia. Antonia had told reporters at an earlier protest that she would be arrested and today she carried out her plans. Greenpeace was present but today they stayed in the background with the rest of the 40 to 50 people who attended. Also arrested was Maria Gracia, 54 who said her husband Jose had almost died from liver problems which she blamed on the dump site. Although she had never been arrested before she said she was prepared to be taken into custody and was arrested several minutes later after she spoke to the reporter. The next day in the Santa Barbara Newspress Antonia was featured on the front page in a large photo being gingerly and carefully placed in the police car. I actually cried when I saw this photo as this was personal to me.

At the same time this protest got underway in Casmalia 20 Greenpeace members entered the federal Environmental Protection Agency office in San Francisco, " to pass out a flyer and press release announcing the citizens of Casmalia were beginning to blockade the dump to enforce the EPA order that the EPA has refused to enforce," said Greenpeace spokesman Bradly Angel. Again, I was hopeful that the Cranston event and the protest arrests would put additional pressure on the EPA because I truly thought are best and final hope lay with the federal government.

HUNTER'S COLLAPSING WORLD

The dump owner's world appeared to be slowly closing in on him with the confluence of numerous events such as the $6.2 million dollar fine from the EPA, the various effective protests by Casmalia residents and allies, the State Water Board's fine of $130,000, the efforts of the county to place reasonable regulations on the dump after the State Supreme Court ruling allowing them to do so and in particular the dump owner's personal problems with his wife's trial in San Diego. Add to all these factors the fact that the judge the good friend of the dump owner was no longer on any Casmalia related cases, and the world was changing for the Hunter scam. All of these items were making it extremely difficult for the owner to push for a new, so called, modernization plan for his toxic dump site.

Conflicting orders from different agencies impacted the dump as well as Hunter's ability to manipulate various regulators. In October of 1989 the Regional Water Board voted 6-2 to close the solid waste landfills to all solid waste, but voted to allow the site to import liquid waste to supposedly help with the solidification process. The County of Santa Barbara wanted testing done on the solidification process before allowing the importation of additional waste for any purpose. Two tests later performed with toxic waste did solidify, but the county said the results were inconclusive and wanted more testing.

In January of 1990 48 test samples were taken and all failed testing. Only four mixtures appeared to harden, but even those using non-toxic materials did not pass the next step called the paint filter test. County officials wanted additional test run using other material, but Casmalia Resources refused to turn over gunk samples of the hazardous seepage to use in the testing. The county was scheduled to go to court again to get the material. The dump owner's new attorney, Fred Fudacz, had a humorous comment to make about the upcoming court confrontation, "We're in a position where they could ask for chocolate fudge to be tested or marshmallow cream to be tested". But the comment did point out the weakness of their position as he did not point out that none of the prior 48 tests showed that the new solidification process worked. If all the expense and money was used to solidify the waste it would still be leaking into the groundwater. At this point it was an ineffective proposal that would just worsen the problem. It was wise of the county to stand firm.

In a Santa Maria Court, the county won a round in the battle to keep Casmalia Resources from using more toxic waste to help clean up the existing toxic waste. They were all set to go to court on March 19, but on March 3 Casmalia Resources notified the county that in 72 hours they would be importing chemicals to start the process. They felt they had orders to do so from the State Health Services and the Regional Water Board. County attorney Jed Beebe immediately sought a restraining order. In granting the restraining order the judge stated, "Taking a little bit more time now to change the system so it doesn't require toxic materials might be the best thing. It seems to me there is a degree of danger that has been presented by the county." So, pressure was added to Hunter's attempts to keep bringing toxic waste and funds to the site.

It was interesting to note what Jed Beebe said, "The county is using the PRC Environmental Management Company to do our testing of the BLS system, but if it is not approved it would appear, they have not explored other methods of cleanup. They've really depended on BLS, and alternatives don't really seem to have been explored"

As far back as 1988-89 the EPA was saying that Casmalia was not qualified for a new permit because of the lack of information they had provided with the application. The EPA contended that they had failed to adequately define the extent of ground water contamination, had not done a thorough enough job in characterizing the flow of ground water under the site, had not submitted an acceptable plan to deal with the storage of rain water, had not designed an adequate monitoring system to facilitate early detection of ground water contamination, failed to identify the concentrations of chemical contaminants, and failed to investigate the fractures in rocks that could let water flow northeast toward the Santa Maria Valley. On top of all this the site was issued the $6.2 million fine for overfilling the site just to keep the money flowing.

HUNTER WANTS TO SELL

Rumors started to fly at the end of 1989 that Hunter was looking to sell the site, but the prospective buyer, although big, had a poor and spotty toxic waste record. Nothing to write home about to say the least. A Browning Ferris Industries, Inc. (BFI) subsidiary, CECOS, was negotiating to buy the problem-plagued Casmalia Resources hazardous waste landfill. In July the company signed a letter of intent to buy the site if it was cleaned up and permits were issued for expansion plans. But, the problems of a small Louisiana farming community called Willow Springs sounded much like those of Casmalia's. CECOS owned the neighboring toxic dump site. Chickens and birds would fall dead out of trees. The dump site fumes made people lethargic and nauseated. At times it was so powerful that it forced them to flee their homes to escape it. Herbert Rigmaiden, who owned a neighboring cattle ranch said, "It made a lot of people pass out and the disposal operation was the culprit." Like Casmalia the people of Willow Springs were suing the dump site and the EPA was also suing, but all the suits were still pending. Most of the folks who live in Willow Springs were black and poor. Poor people, it seemed, were the target and get dumped on by these scams.

The BFI subsidiary's record included many violations around the entire United States. In 1988 they agreed to pay $2.5 million to settle an EPA lawsuit at another Louisiana toxic waste site that had more than 1,700 violations. Rainwater collected in a hazardous waste burial pit in Williamsbur, Ohio was pumped into a creek upstream from the towns water supply. Two employees and the company were indicted by a grand jury. The list of BFI fines and violations went on and on. BFI touted, as Hunter did, that they were "the solution to toxic waste disposal problems and not the problem." Like Hunter locally, BFI could boast of its income as nationwide they brought in $1.3 billion in 1986, $1.6 billion in 1987, and $2 billion in 1988. It was a company and new neighbor we could do without in Santa Barbara County. The good news about the report was that Hunter was growing weaker and less sure of himself and wanted out.

NANCY IS SENTENCED

Kenneth Hunter, in March of 1990, was sitting in the San Diego court room with other family members, prohibited from communicating with his wife Nancy, when he received another blow to his ego. I would have loved to have been present, but had other family obligations. The federal judge rebuffed Nancy Hoover Hunter's tearful plea for mercy and sentenced the onetime San Diego socialite and politician to 10 years in prison for tax evasion arising from her relationship with convicted swindler J. David "Jerry" Dominelli. Nancy Hunter also faced unresolved additional charges.

Nancy Hunter's well-orchestrated plea for mercy went something like this, " I'm terribly sorry for all the pain and suffering I've caused," she sobbed. "I feel very stupid and I feel like my whole life has been a failure. I've tried to find words for the incredible shame I feel. I feel like everything I've done has been wiped out. I'm truly sorry, your honor, and I ask for your mercy."

The one-time mayor of Del Mar and now resident of Montecito knew how to lay it on thick, but the judge wisely rejected this dog and pony show. Eventually Kenneth Hunter, with his vast sums of money, was able to get the sentence reduced to three years, but all these events, I am sure, wore him down both mentally and financially. Unfortunately, wealthy people can play the legal system.

GRADING WORK WITH NO PERMITS

As is usual for the dump site, they take action first and then worry about getting permits.

Toru Miyoshi after it was reported to the board, sends a letter to the State Health Services Director Kenneth Kizer stating, "Our concern stems from recent activities at the dump site, some of which appear to be related to the proposed modernization plan. Permits have not been issued for these activities, nor does there seem to be active onsite regulatory overview. The dump has been proceeding with its proposed modernization plan without the use of county or state permits. As you know the modernization plan consists of a wastewater treatment plant, five lined storage ponds and a large, lined landfill. Site officials have been applying for a county conditional use permit since early this year." The letter demanded that the DHS update the county on the regulation of onsite activities. Also, county attorney Jed Beebe said, "I will be coordinating with the district attorney in filing a public nuisance suit against the site because they have failed to truck its generated onsite waste offsite to a different toxic waste dump site." So, the county was tightening the screws slowly but surely.

SETTLEMENT MAY BE NEAR

In mid-March of 1990 Fred Fudacz, the Casmalia Resource Attorney, announced "settlement was in the works and chances of an agreement seem more likely. We're talking about a settlement and haven't one yet. They're like baseball talks, it's going to be back and forth." Fedacz and several attorneys representing the Casmalia folks met in court that week to continue a change of venue hearing. Now the transferring of venue would take a backseat to settlement talks. He did not comment on what was holding up the talks.

Richard Brenneman, an attorney for the small town of Casmalia said he had not been told of a settlement, but added that he wouldn't know about one until it was presented to him by the other side. He went on to say, "The insurance companies will have to talk amongst themselves and try to work out something and there are more than 25 insurance firms who have represented Casmalia Resources through the years. There must be a meeting of the minds of what responsibility they each have before they can settle the case. Any settlement is meaningless as to how they will share the liability. So, there is one defendant, but many insurance companies." I felt this report was further good news that things were finally winding down. It was also interesting that this talk of settlement and change from venue issues occurred after the dump owner's good friend, Judge Lewellen, was off all Casmalia related cases.

DESERTING THE SINKING SHIP

Employees at Casmalia Toxic dump were slowly being terminated. First, in July 1989 twelve employees were laid off or about 20 percent of the workforce. Then, in November of 1989 when the site shut down because it no longer met new government regulations, more workers were laid off and terminated. Then during December 1990 all employees were laid off except three. When this was announced Hunter was out of town and General Manager Jim McBride was not expected at the office until the next day. Spokesperson Jan Lachenmaier said she was among those who had been laid off and she declined to answer questions put to her by a reporter.

It took until March 1991 for it to dawn on regulators what was in the works. Strangely, the first agency to wake up was the Local State Water Board. Board member Curtis Tunnell of Santa Maria said at the regular meeting, "We've treated Casmalia with kid gloves for way too long. We're fools if we don't see what's happening here—the man is abandoning a site that's no longer financially attractive. He only has three or four employees on site, and his key people, his trained engineers, are now running an environmental testing lab in Santa Maria with Mr. Hunter's money…he's stepped on the other side of the line." The meeting was held in Lompoc and the board reviewed

Casmalia because the staff had become increasingly worried about the cleanup efforts at the closed-down toxics dump. Hunter had stopped paying county permit processing fees and also stopped paying its toxic pit closure report fees to the water board. As a result, its bill had reached up to $130,000. Casmalia Resources had also sold off almost all of its heavy equipment and stopped pumping contaminated ground water underneath its old landfills into trenches as ordered. Staffer Eric Gobler said, "…our major concern is that they are not pumping leachate (contaminated ground water) out of the landfills. There are potentially several hundred thousand gallons of highly contaminated ground water in the old solvent pesticides landfill and in reality, they should be pumping and disposing of it for a long period of time." All board members agreed and voted to ask the state Attorney General to force Casmalia Resources to pay the $130,000 delinquent fees and also voted to urge state and federal agencies to crack down on the dump's cleanup efforts. But the Water Board's wake up as to what was occurring, I was sure, was too little too late as usual!

TWO FIRMS EXPRESS INTEREST IN BUYING

In a February 1991 update meeting in Santa Maria sponsored by the EPA and the state health department, it was pointed out that two firms had expressed interest in the site and have asked specific questions about the site. One was ENSR, a consortium of several firms including Canonie Environmental, Chemfix, American Nu-Kem and a German firm. The other interested firm was Eco-Waste Technologies based in Texas.

Other news was that the Air Pollution Control District had issued a permit for a larger pump needed to extract contaminated liquid. The EPA was still pursuing the $6.2 million fine for exceeding dump capacity. A violation of permit effort has been started for allowing its liability insurance to lapse has been referred to the EPA for possible action. Also the site was now down to two employees as Jim McBride, the general manager, was now gone.

State Senator Gary Hart D-Santa Barbar/Ventura summed up the current situation the best and said, "I find the laundry list of layoffs, equipment sales and insurance woes extremely alarming. The worst fear is that adequate monies may not be in place for needed cleanup and closure of the site."

CHAPTER 21

SETTLEMENT, POLITICS, AND THE AFTERMATH

COMMUNITY LAWSUIT SETTLED

In January 1991 after more than five years of legal wrangling and amongst rumors of dump bankruptcy the community's legal action finally came to an end and I gave a big sigh of relief. It had been a long, grueling, and tense period in my life which had taken me away from my family and normal life. It was good to think I would be away from my all too frequent TV news interviews as well as my almost continuous confrontations with one person or another. I have, however, never regretted the toes I had to step on as all those folks greatly deserved my scorn.

During the prior year my wife and I had managed to make a real estate offer for a ranch that was in bankruptcy in the Cuyama Valley in eastern Santa Barbara County. I was always on the lookout for a good deal in real estate. Cuyama is another Chumash Indian name as are many names along the central California coast. Unlike the wet coastal areas, this is a high desert valley with the rugged, hot, and barren Caliente range on the North-East side of the valley. The ranch sat in the rolling foothills on the back side of the coastal range. When we trudged up the hill on the cattle ranch and turned and looked out over the valley and the rugged mountain range, we both immediately knew that this was the spot and view for our eventual get-away home site. Toward the back of the property was a cave with Indian paintings and a spring that once had an Indian village next to it. We made haste to get our offer in and later the bankruptcy judge agreed to the sale. It was now ours and it was a perfect spot to get away from it all with our two kids!

After more than five years of fighting for retribution the news of the pending settlement spread like wildfire through the community and the attorneys made arrangements by sending out notices for a community meeting in the school's large multi-purpose room. It was made clear that as part of the settlement we would have to agree not to ever mention the exact amount of the settlement. This was fine with me because I just wanted it to be over with.

Although rumors of dump site bankruptcy still hung in the air, Casmalia resident's settlement funds would be coming from insurance companies that had insured the site through the years. But the folks in Casmalia, after their fresh court victory and court approval of the settlement, had a decision to make: Was the financial settlement adequate compensation for what they have experienced, or would they take further action and reject the offer? Only the over 300 plaintiffs could make the decision. When reporters called me about the settlement I explained, "…as part of the settlement residents were ordered to not talk to the press regarding the case, under penalty of libel and nullification of the settlement. The general attitude here regarding the settlement is a happy one, although I don't feel any amount of money can compensate these people for what they've gone through." The amount of the settlement which was arrived at Dec. 31 in Los Angeles County was not being disclosed and a veil of silence now enveloped the entire town. Attorney Brenneman said, "The case was eventually moved to Los Angeles in early 1990 because the defendants said they couldn't get a fair trial in Santa Barbara County. This settlement means that they are vindicated in what the plaintiffs were saying. It also shows to state government and other communities that people can stand up and say something when fumes and chemicals are going onto their property. I think the government has learned something about these things and these kinds of situations from the settlement." I tried to get people in Casmalia to take the settlement. I saw no advantage to dragging this out any further.

After and during the meeting at the school the vast majority voted to accept the settlement. The attorneys present explained that a retired judge would be used to divide up the settlement proceeds among the plaintiffs and £hat he would use one of the classrooms in the evenings to meet with plaintiffs one at a time as needed. Eventually, all the paper work was completed and each plaintiff received his or her check in the mail and the lawsuit was over. Those who had been trapped in Casmalia now had the where with all to move on if they wished to do so. The complete collapse of the scam was imminent. We were on the verge of completely, "Closing it, capping it, and cleaning it up." All the fantasies that kept funds rolling into the dump site had been proven wrong. No longer did a wall of resistance exist.

POLITICAL OPPORTUNITY

After the plane trip to Sacramento my son and I were picked up and we rode with Kathie Hoxie to the capitol steps and on the drive she and her sister spent the news of the departure of one of our local representatives. This they thought would give someone an early edge for the seat because it was not common knowledge. It was interesting, but had no deep meaning to me.

Later after the settlement I was asked to meet with three people including Kathie to discuss a possible run by me for this soon-to-be-vacant office. I had been highly visible for almost six years on TV and other media. It did make sense as my name and appearance had been hammered into the California Central Coast memory. So, I responded with a question after they asked, "Where would we get the money from to finance the venture?" They said they would work on that part. We left it at I would have to think about it for a few days. I was certainly flattered that they thought of me and that I now knew the long-ago conversation in the auto was partly for my benefit, but this would require some serious thought on my part. I was tired of being in the public spot light and longed to spend time with my children and family. I knew this would be another long and arduous undertaking. So, I opted for a home life with the family and eventually thanked them all for the thought, as the political life was not for me—it would be too much like the last few years that now seemed like an entire lifetime.

THE AFTERMATH OF THE STRUGGLE

The major players, in the drama that had unfolded after the first threatening letter to me, all went their separate ways after the settlement. Hunter did not go into bankruptcy, but in 1991 he did walk away and abandon the dump site as the various regulators closed all the doors to additional income. The EPA, after abandonment, moved in and took control over the site. In early 1992 it became an official superfund site. Finally, in 2002 a settlement was reached with Casmalia Resources that provided for a $7 million cleanup fine plus Casmalia Resources waived any claim to the $13 million Closure/Post-Closure trust Fund. Jane Diamond of the Superfund Office said, "In reaching our second settlement in the past six month we are working to ensure that we will have the money necessary to devise and implement a long-term, protective cleanup."

Lawsuits continued for years. U.S. Assistant Attorney General Tom Sansonetti said, "The settlement represents our continuing efforts to ensure those responsible for contamination share in the costs of the cleanup. We will continue to focus on the remaining liable parties who have dumped materials at the site."

Immediately after the EPA moved in and the site was being properly capped the community's respiratory problems as well as mine started to dissipate. I had zero respiratory problems in the next five years. Also, after the settlement, at the same time, the strange static on all the opponent's phone lines strangely vanished. The community was returning to normal.

Dr. Lawrence Hart now 61, the Santa Barbara County Health Department Director, remains to this day a mystery to me as to his motivations, but he and his department did benefit from the settlement and the EPA actions. Was he truly motivated by good will or did the bomb threat and the billion-dollar law suit by the community move him and the Board of Supervisors toward actually extending a helping hand to us all? No one will ever know, but we are all indebted to the efforts of Jed Beebe, the young attorney, who carried the ball for the county in attempting to regulate the dump site.

Dr. Hart ran into tough times as health director at the end of 1989 and the beginning of 1990. There were rumors flying that he was seeking a new position in either Hawaii or San Francisco. Luckily for him all of his subordinates in the Air Pollution District who had been directly responsible for the negligent supervision and regulation of the toxic dump site were long gone, either voluntarily or otherwise, but the buck does stop at the top and to this day I take great offence to the lies and cover up early on to me about the cyanide exposure that endangered both me and the school children under my care. Dr. Hart at $115,000 per year was the highest paid county official at the time in Santa Barbara County, so the county had a right to expect more. A grand jury report was about to be issued and Supervisor Bill Wallace said, "They (The health department) have been charging a lot for environmental toxic health inspections fees and not later doing all the work, and putting the money somewhere else. The environmental health section is really limping along right now." Hart had sent letters to each supervisor asking for an appointment to discuss personnel matters. "I think he is fishing to see how much support he has with the board. There are a lot of rumblings", said an official. Talk had been rife during the past months about Hart's possible departure and Hart readily admitted these events. But one thing did occur to strengthen Dr. Hart's position as the dump site closed and settlement was reached. The county was let off the hook on the community's pending lawsuit. They did deserve some recognition for Jed Beebe's efforts and the county's efforts to finally regulate the site.

Nancy Hoover Hunter ended up serving just three of her ten-year-sentence. Kenneth Hunter, the dump owner and her husband, eventually died after spending about $2 to $3 million on her legal fees. Then, Nancy Hunter re-married Eugene Fletcher and they have homes in Rancho Santa Fe, Coronado Cays and also have access to a Del Mar beach home used by her husband's clan. At last report they were building another home in Mexico.

The Casmalia community's legal team of attorneys all continued with successful legal careers. Attorney Jed Beebe eventually became a superior court judge in Santa Barbara County. Former Judge Lewellen continued on where he belonged in retirement. Supervisor Toru Miyoshi completed two full distinguished terms as a supervisor and should be proud of standing up for the underdog and what was right. Former Supervisor DeWayne Holmdal went into retirement after his defeat and was never heard from again by anyone known to me. Not ever hearing of him again "made my day" through the following years, but after many, many years and after voters' memories faded he was able to land a seat on the Lompoc City Council and in a flash was being investigated by the District Attorney for violations of the California State Open Meetings Laws. Again, and as usual he had outlandish and irrational comments to make about the investigation by law enforcement!

Jerry Corlew and his wife and small child almost immediately moved to Lake Isabella in Kern County where he bought a home and continued his fishing lure business next to the lake. He was free at last. Nick Irmiter and his family stayed in Casmalia for a few more years, but eventually purchased a new home in Orcutt. He later started working for the court system as a court conservator. His wife Angie continued as a nurse at the local hospital. Kenneth Vaniter, and his wife, Philis, stayed in Casmalia, they said, "because this is our home." Kathy Hoxie continued working for non-profits and kept her interest in politics. Joyce Howerton eventually became the mayor of Lompoc. Bradly Angel with Greenpeace continued his efforts to save the environment. It now seemed safe in Casmalia so some stayed, but some moved quickly away. It seemed that the old timers with long time roots in the community were more likely to stay, but we had all accomplished our mutual goals of "Closing it, capping it, and cleaning it up." Perseverance had paid off!

I had never planned on making my life occupation the small rural school, but after this six-year toxic dump period I did not have long to go until retirement age so I decided to continue on at Wollam Elementary School.

The next four years of my life were the most fulfilling for me. I immediately tried to spend more time with my family and on weekends we would go up and camp out in a trailer on our new ranch property in the Cuyama Valley. The entire family worked on building a new large barn on the property. By then our daughter Meghan was 7 and our son John was 10 when we started on this project. Being the optimist that I usually am on projects I envisioned that the 2,500 SF barn would be done in a flash. John and I headed up to put on the new roofing after it was delivered. I can remember looking down at John and his terrified face as I started up on the scissor lift taking up the new truss to set in place. It was at the moment that I realized that we needed the help of a contractor. So, I made some quick phone calls and he and his crew were available and the roof completed in no time that weekend. Life was good and we later constructed a bunk house and tack shack on the property.

But as I approached the age of 55 or so I had what I thought were minor health problems. I needed some surgery that was to be done through arthroscopy, in about 1-2 hours, it ended up taking almost 5 hours in the operating room. The next morning, I awoke with my wife standing over me and I was so weak that I found I could not even lift my hand or arm. I had a severe case of pneumonia. They showed me the instrument to suck from to exercise your lungs, but to put it bluntly I was so weak I did not give a shit and preferred to be left alone to die as I was so weak and tired. It was a totally new experience for me to feel this way, but I later found it is common with sever pneumonia. My wife and my brother-in-law Tom were to have none of this. They insisted that I get up out of bed and walk. So off I went with them pushing along all my wired attachments on the portable hospital cart. One came in the morning and the other in the afternoon for this routine.

It was at this time in the hallway that I met a familiar face. It was a teacher that worked at my school who to my surprise was pushing along the same regalia of medical attachments. She was the one who had helped me shut down the school. We both hardly acknowledged each other because of our weakened conditions. I later found that she had been admitted for lung cancer and she passed away shortly after our passing each other in the hallway. Another case of lung cancer for Casmalia.

After a few days of antibiotics and this walking, which exercised my lungs, I slowly got somewhat better and after seven days the doctors wanted me to go home so I would not catch an infection from just being in the hospital. At home I had a hospital bed and was still hooked up to all the lines plus a visiting nurse. But at the end of my week at home I started to develop a high temperature, so it was back to the hospital I went.

I was then diagnosed with a case of pancreatitis. In my new hospital room, a pick was placed next to my heart so they could feed me through my veins. The plan was to let my stomach and pancreas rest for a week. It was then the doctor explained to me about the nodules that had formed in my pancreas and if they kept getting larger and grew together, I would die. If they started to get smaller, I would get better and survive. Most people die with this condition, but I was lucky and the nodules got smaller. We never told our own children or my co-workers at school that I had had two near death experiences.

Eventually, I again returned home to recuperate. It had been quite an ordeal and I had lost 30 pounds. It was quite a hit to my entire body. I stayed home for about two months and then returned to work for the last two months of the school year. I knew I might have made the wrong decision about returning to work when a teacher's aide met me the first day in front of the building to explain to me her side of a school dispute and wanting me to decide the issue. She did not know at the time that a small breeze would have blown me over!

I limped through the school year, but after the school year ended I was required as the Principal/Superintendent to attend an adversarial type hearing at the county school's office in Santa Barbara to represent the school district's position. I did fine at the hearing, but it was extremely wearing on me. On the drive home I realized that I was in over my head both mentally and physically and that I was not fit enough to continue on.

I first stopped at my parents' home to let them know that I had decided to retire early, but was concerned about the upcoming expenses of our children's college education. They volunteered to help out if needed and I should not worry. Luckily, I had reached 55 years of age, the first tier of the state teacher's retirement, which provided less than later age retirement, but by this time in our life my obsession with real estate had guaranteed us additional retirement income. After discussions with my wife and doctor, he told me that mental and physical exhaustion was not uncommon for serious illness. I retired after 27 ½ years in the small rural school and community I had grown to love. My secretary, Meg, and the county school's business officials tried to talk me into staying for a few more years, but they did not know how seriously ill I had been. I stayed on during the summer to help the district interview applicants and to find a replacement, but I have never regretted my decision to retire early. After a few years in retirement my health returned robustly and I have had a wonderful retirement.

I hope I am remembered, by all of our adversaries, as the wrong person to send a threatening letter to as it was the spark that started an environmental movement. I did learn one good thing to remember from my many years at the small school and community that tenacity is a good thing and if you are ever confronted by seemingly overwhelming issues dealing with reluctant, arrogant, biased, corrupt, and negligent individuals such as pubic elected officials, regulators, lawyers or judges just stop and repeat Los Angeles Mayor Tom Bradley's old saying and rallying call several times, "I am madder than hell and I am not going to take it any longer".

EPILOGUE

Environmental conditions have changed substantially in the past 30 years and not always for the best environmentally speaking I had a great laugh at a recent commentary that appeared in Santa Barbara County newspapers arguing for less regulation, and that actually tried to convince readers that the United Nations was out to get us all with a conspiracy with the local Air Pollution Control Districts and the Environmental Defense Center. This paranoid view reminded me of Don Quixote charging around the countryside challenging windmills believing they were imaginary dragons.

My mind flashed back to 1984 and I reflected on events when I was forced to close our small school. That event coupled with the threatening letter set off the six-year battle between our small community and the scam that included high powered money interests at the county, state and federal levels. Respiratory illness was rampant in students, staff and community. I can vividly remember the sadness I felt when, Mrs. Davis, our teacher, died from blood disorders. Eventually I worked closely with four law firms, one local firm and three large Los Angeles firms. I helped take the lead and I take much pride in the fact that our small community succeeded in closing the dump site and securing a multi-million-dollar settlement for the community. Dump employees' reaction to my activities ranged from actually trying to kill me to providing me with dump technical information. Working with the United States EPA, we were instrumental in causing the $6 million fine to be levied against the site that speeded the capping of the site and forcing the scam to finally end when the gates closed. So, it is an understatement to say I am sensitive to false and misleading environmental views and opinions.

The cyanide gas reached students under my care because of the greed and influence of California industries plus the lax Santa Barbara County air pollution control supervision that actually allowed the dump owner to operate a machine that was not designed to process cyanide or other toxics for well over six years without regulation or a permit. The off gas containing cyanide and numerous other highly toxic pollutants eventually reached not only Casmalia, but also the entire Orcutt area on the central coast.

The naïve newspaper commentary also challenged the need to control carbon dioxide emissions and seems unaware of a 2010 report issued by the National Academy of Sciences that concluded that 97 percent of scientific experts agreed and concluded that rampant climate change is caused by humans burning fossil fuels. With our constant extremes in temperatures and weather conditions we should all be concerned. I still believe in the lofty goals I set forth early on for the toxic industry, but piled on to those woes we now have human caused climate change with its extremes in weather running the gamut from mega sea storms, drought conditions as well as the slow melting of the world's ice caps and the slow but sure rise in sea levels around the globe. The challenges are immense.

I wish I could report to you that the toxic waste industry and its regulation had improved in the intervening years, but it has, in fact, worsened. A report covered by the Associated Press on December 28, 2013 found that California regulators have allowed dozens of waste facilities to operate with expired permits while reducing enforcement. A quarter of the major hazardous waste sites in the state of California are operating on expired permits. The department has not even tried to collect the $140 million in outstanding fines due since 1987.

I still believe in those lofty goals I laid out in the commentary I wrote in 1986. Casmalia's story is a tragic and graphic example of the failure of local and state control. I strongly feel that national problems deserve national recognition and national solutions. Let us make Casmalia truly the last one—the last poorly run private toxic landfill.

Soon California will be broken down into 19 areas for the purpose of health insurance rates. Insurance companies will set rates using, among other items, the pollution in each area of the state. Statistics have shown the higher the pollution the greater your risk of being ill, therefore, the higher your insurance rate. Environmental issues personally affect each and every one of us.

Chevron Oil Company has taken the lead and sets an example in developing solutions. They have laid out "Seven Principles for Addressing Climate Change" for their company. Local industries, businesses, homes and individuals should be establishing their own plan to reduce their "carbon foot print" on the world stage. Whether it be-- driving less, putting solar on your roof, buying more fuel-efficient autos, insulating your home, or lobbying your representative for hydrogen power research--you do need to get busy on your plan and take individual action.

The Don Quixote approach of charging windmills to blame others does not solve our problems, but working together does. The 1984 local Air Pollution Control District's dismal record of dealing with the tragedy in Casmalia shows us regulators will bend in the wind under pressure and they need our strong support to stand firm and enforce reasonable regulations, but it required communities and the nation need to apply a strong dose of tenacity,

Classified

Santa Barbara News Press

Residents, teachers and students from Casmalia
marched Into the governor's office In Sacramento